# CHARACTER *Development* JOURNAL

**Everything you need to create characters your readers will love!**

## JOURNALS FOR AUTHORS

### SWEET HARMONY PRESS

| Name/Nicknames | | Age/Birthday | Race |
|---|---|---|---|
| Height/Weight | Gender/Sexuality | Eyes | Hair color |
| Parents | | Place of Birth | Species |
| Siblings | | Class/Status | Education |
| Where they have lived | | Schools Attended | |
| Clothes/Glasses/Scars | | Spiritual Beliefs | |
| Occupation | | Awards/Accomplishments | |
| Strongest personality characteristics | | Favorite activities/Hobbies | |
| People they love | | People they hate | |
| People they admire | | Pets | Hobbies |
| Problems | | Dreams and Ambitions | |

| Important role in the story | |
|---|---|
| Past experiences that shaped who they are | |

| Character Arc | Notes |
|---|---|
| | |

- Accountable
- Adaptable
- Adventurous
- Affable
- Alert
- Ambitious
- Appropriate
- Arrogant
- Assertive
- Astute
- Attentive
- Authentic
- Boorish
- Bossy
- Bravery
- Calm
- Candid
- Capable
- Charismatic
- Charming
- Collaborative
- Committed
- Communicator
- Compassionate
- Conceited
- Confident
- Connected
- Conscientious
- Considerate
- Consistent
- Cooperative
- Courageous
- Cowardly
- Creative
- Cultured
- Curious
- Dedicated
- Dependable
- Determined
- Diplomatic
- Disciplined
- Discreet
- Dishonest
- Dutiful
- Easygoing
- Efficient
- Empathetic
- Encouraging
- Energetic
- Enthusiastic
- Ethical
- Expressive
- Exuberant
- Facilitates
- Fair
- Fairness
- Faithful
- Fearless
- Finicky
- Flexible
- Friendly
- Generative
- Generosity
- Gratitude
- Gregarious
- Happy
- Hard-Working
- Helpful
- Honest
- Honorable
- Humble
- Humorous
- Imaginative
- Immaculate
- Impartial
- Impulsive
- Independent
- Inquiring
- Innovative
- Intelligent
- Intentional
- Interested
- Intimate
- Joyful
- Keen
- Knowledgeable
- Lazy
- Listener
- Lively
- Logical
- Loving
- Loyal
- Malicious
- Meticulous
- Networker
- Nurturing
- Obnoxious
- Observant
- Open-Minded
- Optimistic
- Organized
- Patient
- Peaceful
- Persistent
- Picky
- Planner
- Playful
- Poised
- Polite
- Pompous
- Powerful
- Pragmatic
- Precise
- Proactive
- Problem-Solver
- Productive
- Punctual
- Quarrelsome
- Reliable
- Resourceful
- Responsible
- Rude
- Sarcastic
- Self-centered
- Self-confident
- Self-reliant
- Sense of Humor
- Sensual
- Serves Others
- Sincere
- Skillful
- Slovenly
- Sneaky
- Spiritual
- Spontaneous
- Stable
- Stingy
- Strong
- Successful
- Sullen
- Supportive
- Surly
- Tactful
- Thoughtless
- Trusting
- Trusting
- Trustworthy
- Truthful
- Unfriendly
- Unruly
- Versatile
- Vibrant
- Vulgar
- Warm
- Wise
- Zealous

| Name/Nicknames | | Age/Birthday | Race |
|---|---|---|---|
| Height/Weight | Gender/Sexuality | Eyes | Hair color |
| Parents | | Place of Birth | Species |
| Siblings | | Class/Status | Education |
| Where they have lived | | Schools Attended | |
| Clothes/Glasses/Scars | | Spiritual Beliefs | |
| Occupation | | Awards/Accomplishments | |
| Strongest personality characteristics | | Favorite activities/Hobbies | |
| People they love | | People they hate | |
| People they admire | | Pets | Hobbies |
| Problems | | Dreams and Ambitions | |

| Important role in the story | |
|---|---|
| Past experiences that shaped who they are | |

| Character Arc | Notes |
|---|---|
| | |

| | | | |
|---|---|---|---|
| ○ Accountable | ○ Diplomatic | ○ Innovative | ○ Quarrelsome |
| ○ Adaptable | ○ Disciplined | ○ Intelligent | ○ Reliable |
| ○ Adventurous | ○ Discreet | ○ Intentional | ○ Resourceful |
| ○ Affable | ○ Dishonest | ○ Interested | ○ Responsible |
| ○ Alert | ○ Dutiful | ○ Intimate | ○ Rude |
| ○ Ambitious | ○ Easygoing | ○ Joyful | ○ Sarcastic |
| ○ Appropriate | ○ Efficient | ○ Keen | ○ Self-centered |
| ○ Arrogant | ○ Empathetic | ○ Knowledgeable | ○ Self-confident |
| ○ Assertive | ○ Encouraging | ○ Lazy | ○ Self-reliant |
| ○ Astute | ○ Energetic | ○ Listener | ○ Sense of Humor |
| ○ Attentive | ○ Enthusiastic | ○ Lively | ○ Sensual |
| ○ Authentic | ○ Ethical | ○ Logical | ○ Serves Others |
| ○ Boorish | ○ Expressive | ○ Loving | ○ Sincere |
| ○ Bossy | ○ Exuberant | ○ Loyal | ○ Skillful |
| ○ Bravery | ○ Facilitates | ○ Malicious | ○ Slovenly |
| ○ Calm | ○ Fair | ○ Meticulous | ○ Sneaky |
| ○ Candid | ○ Fairness | ○ Networker | ○ Spiritual |
| ○ Capable | ○ Faithful | ○ Nurturing | ○ Spontaneous |
| ○ Charismatic | ○ Fearless | ○ Obnoxious | ○ Stable |
| ○ Charming | ○ Finicky | ○ Observant | ○ Stingy |
| ○ Collaborative | ○ Flexible | ○ Open-Minded | ○ Strong |
| ○ Committed | ○ Friendly | ○ Optimistic | ○ Successful |
| ○ Communicator | ○ Generative | ○ Organized | ○ Sullen |
| ○ Compassionate | ○ Generosity | ○ Patient | ○ Supportive |
| ○ Conceited | ○ Gratitude | ○ Peaceful | ○ Surly |
| ○ Confident | ○ Gregarious | ○ Persistent | ○ Tactful |
| ○ Connected | ○ Happy | ○ Picky | ○ Thoughtless |
| ○ Conscientious | ○ Hard-Working | ○ Planner | ○ Trusting |
| ○ Considerate | ○ Helpful | ○ Playful | ○ Trusting |
| ○ Consistent | ○ Honest | ○ Poised | ○ Trustworthy |
| ○ Cooperative | ○ Honorable | ○ Polite | ○ Truthful |
| ○ Courageous | ○ Humble | ○ Pompous | ○ Unfriendly |
| ○ Cowardly | ○ Humorous | ○ Powerful | ○ Unruly |
| ○ Creative | ○ Imaginative | ○ Pragmatic | ○ Versatile |
| ○ Cultured | ○ Immaculate | ○ Precise | ○ Vibrant |
| ○ Curious | ○ Impartial | ○ Proactive | ○ Vulgar |
| ○ Dedicated | ○ Impulsive | ○ Problem-Solver | ○ Warm |
| ○ Dependable | ○ Independent | ○ Productive | ○ Wise |
| ○ Determined | ○ Inquiring | ○ Punctual | ○ Zealous |

| Name/Nicknames | | Age/Birthday | Race |
| --- | --- | --- | --- |
| Height/Weight | Gender/Sexuality | Eyes | Hair color |
| Parents | | Place of Birth | Species |
| Siblings | | Class/Status | Education |
| Where they have lived | | Schools Attended | |
| Clothes/Glasses/Scars | | Spiritual Beliefs | |
| Occupation | | Awards/Accomplishments | |
| Strongest personality characteristics | | Favorite activities/Hobbies | |
| People they love | | People they hate | |
| People they admire | | Pets | Hobbies |
| Problems | | Dreams and Ambitions | |

| | |
|---|---|
| *Important role in the story* | |
| *Past experiences that shaped who they are* | |
| Character Arc | Notes |

- Accountable
- Adaptable
- Adventurous
- Affable
- Alert
- Ambitious
- Appropriate
- Arrogant
- Assertive
- Astute
- Attentive
- Authentic
- Boorish
- Bossy
- Bravery
- Calm
- Candid
- Capable
- Charismatic
- Charming
- Collaborative
- Committed
- Communicator
- Compassionate
- Conceited
- Confident
- Connected
- Conscientious
- Considerate
- Consistent
- Cooperative
- Courageous
- Cowardly
- Creative
- Cultured
- Curious
- Dedicated
- Dependable
- Determined
- Diplomatic
- Disciplined
- Discreet
- Dishonest
- Dutiful
- Easygoing
- Efficient
- Empathetic
- Encouraging
- Energetic
- Enthusiastic
- Ethical
- Expressive
- Exuberant
- Facilitates
- Fair
- Fairness
- Faithful
- Fearless
- Finicky
- Flexible
- Friendly
- Generative
- Generosity
- Gratitude
- Gregarious
- Happy
- Hard-Working
- Helpful
- Honest
- Honorable
- Humble
- Humorous
- Imaginative
- Immaculate
- Impartial
- Impulsive
- Independent
- Inquiring
- Innovative
- Intelligent
- Intentional
- Interested
- Intimate
- Joyful
- Keen
- Knowledgeable
- Lazy
- Listener
- Lively
- Logical
- Loving
- Loyal
- Malicious
- Meticulous
- Networker
- Nurturing
- Obnoxious
- Observant
- Open-Minded
- Optimistic
- Organized
- Patient
- Peaceful
- Persistent
- Picky
- Planner
- Playful
- Poised
- Polite
- Pompous
- Powerful
- Pragmatic
- Precise
- Proactive
- Problem-Solver
- Productive
- Punctual
- Quarrelsome
- Reliable
- Resourceful
- Responsible
- Rude
- Sarcastic
- Self-centered
- Self-confident
- Self-reliant
- Sense of Humor
- Sensual
- Serves Others
- Sincere
- Skillful
- Slovenly
- Sneaky
- Spiritual
- Spontaneous
- Stable
- Stingy
- Strong
- Successful
- Sullen
- Supportive
- Surly
- Tactful
- Thoughtless
- Trusting
- Trusting
- Trustworthy
- Truthful
- Unfriendly
- Unruly
- Versatile
- Vibrant
- Vulgar
- Warm
- Wise
- Zealous

| Name/Nicknames | | Age/Birthday | Race |
|---|---|---|---|
| Height/Weight | Gender/Sexuality | Eyes | Hair color |
| Parents | | Place of Birth | Species |
| Siblings | | Class/Status | Education |
| Where they have lived | | Schools Attended | |
| Clothes/Glasses/Scars | | Spiritual Beliefs | |
| Occupation | | Awards/Accomplishments | |
| Strongest personality characteristics | | Favorite activities/Hobbies | |
| People they love | | People they hate | |
| People they admire | | Pets | Hobbies |
| Problems | | Dreams and Ambitions | |

| Important role in the story | | | |
|---|---|---|---|
| Past experiences that shaped who they are | | | |
| Character Arc | | Notes | |

| | | | | | | | |
|---|---|---|---|---|---|---|---|
| o | Accountable | o | Diplomatic | o | Innovative | o | Quarrelsome |
| o | Adaptable | o | Disciplined | o | Intelligent | o | Reliable |
| o | Adventurous | o | Discreet | o | Intentional | o | Resourceful |
| o | Affable | o | Dishonest | o | Interested | o | Responsible |
| o | Alert | o | Dutiful | o | Intimate | o | Rude |
| o | Ambitious | o | Easygoing | o | Joyful | o | Sarcastic |
| o | Appropriate | o | Efficient | o | Keen | o | Self-centered |
| o | Arrogant | o | Empathetic | o | Knowledgeable | o | Self-confident |
| o | Assertive | o | Encouraging | o | Lazy | o | Self-reliant |
| o | Astute | o | Energetic | o | Listener | o | Sense of Humor |
| o | Attentive | o | Enthusiastic | o | Lively | o | Sensual |
| o | Authentic | o | Ethical | o | Logical | o | Serves Others |
| o | Boorish | o | Expressive | o | Loving | o | Sincere |
| o | Bossy | o | Exuberant | o | Loyal | o | Skillful |
| o | Bravery | o | Facilitates | o | Malicious | o | Slovenly |
| o | Calm | o | Fair | o | Meticulous | o | Sneaky |
| o | Candid | o | Fairness | o | Networker | o | Spiritual |
| o | Capable | o | Faithful | o | Nurturing | o | Spontaneous |
| o | Charismatic | o | Fearless | o | Obnoxious | o | Stable |
| o | Charming | o | Finicky | o | Observant | o | Stingy |
| o | Collaborative | o | Flexible | o | Open-Minded | o | Strong |
| o | Committed | o | Friendly | o | Optimistic | o | Successful |
| o | Communicator | o | Generative | o | Organized | o | Sullen |
| o | Compassionate | o | Generosity | o | Patient | o | Supportive |
| o | Conceited | o | Gratitude | o | Peaceful | o | Surly |
| o | Confident | o | Gregarious | o | Persistent | o | Tactful |
| o | Connected | o | Happy | o | Picky | o | Thoughtless |
| o | Conscientious | o | Hard-Working | o | Planner | o | Trusting |
| o | Considerate | o | Helpful | o | Playful | o | Trusting |
| o | Consistent | o | Honest | o | Poised | o | Trustworthy |
| o | Cooperative | o | Honorable | o | Polite | o | Truthful |
| o | Courageous | o | Humble | o | Pompous | o | Unfriendly |
| o | Cowardly | o | Humorous | o | Powerful | o | Unruly |
| o | Creative | o | Imaginative | o | Pragmatic | o | Versatile |
| o | Cultured | o | Immaculate | o | Precise | o | Vibrant |
| o | Curious | o | Impartial | o | Proactive | o | Vulgar |
| o | Dedicated | o | Impulsive | o | Problem-Solver | o | Warm |
| o | Dependable | o | Independent | o | Productive | o | Wise |
| o | Determined | o | Inquiring | o | Punctual | o | Zealous |

| Name/Nicknames | | Age/Birthday | Race |
|---|---|---|---|
| Height/Weight | Gender/Sexuality | Eyes | Hair color |
| Parents | | Place of Birth | Species |
| Siblings | | Class/Status | Education |
| Where they have lived | | Schools Attended | |
| Clothes/Glasses/Scars | | Spiritual Beliefs | |
| Occupation | | Awards/Accomplishments | |
| Strongest personality characteristics | | Favorite activities/Hobbies | |
| People they love | | People they hate | |
| People they admire | | Pets | Hobbies |
| Problems | | Dreams and Ambitions | |

| Important role in the story | |
|---|---|
| Past experiences that shaped who they are | |
| Character Arc | Notes |

| | | | | | | | |
|---|---|---|---|---|---|---|---|
| o | Accountable | o | Diplomatic | o | Innovative | o | Quarrelsome |
| o | Adaptable | o | Disciplined | o | Intelligent | o | Reliable |
| o | Adventurous | o | Discreet | o | Intentional | o | Resourceful |
| o | Affable | o | Dishonest | o | Interested | o | Responsible |
| o | Alert | o | Dutiful | o | Intimate | o | Rude |
| o | Ambitious | o | Easygoing | o | Joyful | o | Sarcastic |
| o | Appropriate | o | Efficient | o | Keen | o | Self-centered |
| o | Arrogant | o | Empathetic | o | Knowledgeable | o | Self-confident |
| o | Assertive | o | Encouraging | o | Lazy | o | Self-reliant |
| o | Astute | o | Energetic | o | Listener | o | Sense of Humor |
| o | Attentive | o | Enthusiastic | o | Lively | o | Sensual |
| o | Authentic | o | Ethical | o | Logical | o | Serves Others |
| o | Boorish | o | Expressive | o | Loving | o | Sincere |
| o | Bossy | o | Exuberant | o | Loyal | o | Skillful |
| o | Bravery | o | Facilitates | o | Malicious | o | Slovenly |
| o | Calm | o | Fair | o | Meticulous | o | Sneaky |
| o | Candid | o | Fairness | o | Networker | o | Spiritual |
| o | Capable | o | Faithful | o | Nurturing | o | Spontaneous |
| o | Charismatic | o | Fearless | o | Obnoxious | o | Stable |
| o | Charming | o | Finicky | o | Observant | o | Stingy |
| o | Collaborative | o | Flexible | o | Open-Minded | o | Strong |
| o | Committed | o | Friendly | o | Optimistic | o | Successful |
| o | Communicator | o | Generative | o | Organized | o | Sullen |
| o | Compassionate | o | Generosity | o | Patient | o | Supportive |
| o | Conceited | o | Gratitude | o | Peaceful | o | Surly |
| o | Confident | o | Gregarious | o | Persistent | o | Tactful |
| o | Connected | o | Happy | o | Picky | o | Thoughtless |
| o | Conscientious | o | Hard-Working | o | Planner | o | Trusting |
| o | Considerate | o | Helpful | o | Playful | o | Trusting |
| o | Consistent | o | Honest | o | Poised | o | Trustworthy |
| o | Cooperative | o | Honorable | o | Polite | o | Truthful |
| o | Courageous | o | Humble | o | Pompous | o | Unfriendly |
| o | Cowardly | o | Humorous | o | Powerful | o | Unruly |
| o | Creative | o | Imaginative | o | Pragmatic | o | Versatile |
| o | Cultured | o | Immaculate | o | Precise | o | Vibrant |
| o | Curious | o | Impartial | o | Proactive | o | Vulgar |
| o | Dedicated | o | Impulsive | o | Problem-Solver | o | Warm |
| o | Dependable | o | Independent | o | Productive | o | Wise |
| o | Determined | o | Inquiring | o | Punctual | o | Zealous |

| Name/Nicknames | | Age/Birthday | Race |
|---|---|---|---|
| Height/Weight | Gender/Sexuality | Eyes | Hair color |
| Parents | | Place of Birth | Species |
| Siblings | | Class/Status | Education |
| Where they have lived | | Schools Attended | |
| Clothes/Glasses/Scars | | Spiritual Beliefs | |
| Occupation | | Awards/Accomplishments | |
| Strongest personality characteristics | | Favorite activities/Hobbies | |
| People they love | | People they hate | |
| People they admire | | Pets | Hobbies |
| Problems | | Dreams and Ambitions | |

| Important role in the story | |
|---|---|
| Past experiences that shaped who they are | |

| Character Arc | Notes |
|---|---|
| | |

| | | | | | | | |
|---|---|---|---|---|---|---|---|
| o | Accountable | o | Diplomatic | o | Innovative | o | Quarrelsome |
| o | Adaptable | o | Disciplined | o | Intelligent | o | Reliable |
| o | Adventurous | o | Discreet | o | Intentional | o | Resourceful |
| o | Affable | o | Dishonest | o | Interested | o | Responsible |
| o | Alert | o | Dutiful | o | Intimate | o | Rude |
| o | Ambitious | o | Easygoing | o | Joyful | o | Sarcastic |
| o | Appropriate | o | Efficient | o | Keen | o | Self-centered |
| o | Arrogant | o | Empathetic | o | Knowledgeable | o | Self-confident |
| o | Assertive | o | Encouraging | o | Lazy | o | Self-reliant |
| o | Astute | o | Energetic | o | Listener | o | Sense of Humor |
| o | Attentive | o | Enthusiastic | o | Lively | o | Sensual |
| o | Authentic | o | Ethical | o | Logical | o | Serves Others |
| o | Boorish | o | Expressive | o | Loving | o | Sincere |
| o | Bossy | o | Exuberant | o | Loyal | o | Skillful |
| o | Bravery | o | Facilitates | o | Malicious | o | Slovenly |
| o | Calm | o | Fair | o | Meticulous | o | Sneaky |
| o | Candid | o | Fairness | o | Networker | o | Spiritual |
| o | Capable | o | Faithful | o | Nurturing | o | Spontaneous |
| o | Charismatic | o | Fearless | o | Obnoxious | o | Stable |
| o | Charming | o | Finicky | o | Observant | o | Stingy |
| o | Collaborative | o | Flexible | o | Open-Minded | o | Strong |
| o | Committed | o | Friendly | o | Optimistic | o | Successful |
| o | Communicator | o | Generative | o | Organized | o | Sullen |
| o | Compassionate | o | Generosity | o | Patient | o | Supportive |
| o | Conceited | o | Gratitude | o | Peaceful | o | Surly |
| o | Confident | o | Gregarious | o | Persistent | o | Tactful |
| o | Connected | o | Happy | o | Picky | o | Thoughtless |
| o | Conscientious | o | Hard-Working | o | Planner | o | Trusting |
| o | Considerate | o | Helpful | o | Playful | o | Trusting |
| o | Consistent | o | Honest | o | Poised | o | Trustworthy |
| o | Cooperative | o | Honorable | o | Polite | o | Truthful |
| o | Courageous | o | Humble | o | Pompous | o | Unfriendly |
| o | Cowardly | o | Humorous | o | Powerful | o | Unruly |
| o | Creative | o | Imaginative | o | Pragmatic | o | Versatile |
| o | Cultured | o | Immaculate | o | Precise | o | Vibrant |
| o | Curious | o | Impartial | o | Proactive | o | Vulgar |
| o | Dedicated | o | Impulsive | o | Problem-Solver | o | Warm |
| o | Dependable | o | Independent | o | Productive | o | Wise |
| o | Determined | o | Inquiring | o | Punctual | o | Zealous |

| Name/Nicknames | | Age/Birthday | Race |
|---|---|---|---|
| Height/Weight | Gender/Sexuality | Eyes | Hair color |
| Parents | | Place of Birth | Species |
| Siblings | | Class/Status | Education |
| Where they have lived | | Schools Attended | |
| Clothes/Glasses/Scars | | Spiritual Beliefs | |
| Occupation | | Awards/Accomplishments | |
| Strongest personality characteristics | | Favorite activities/Hobbies | |
| People they love | | People they hate | |
| People they admire | | Pets | Hobbies |
| Problems | | Dreams and Ambitions | |

| Important role in the story | |
|---|---|
| Past experiences that shaped who they are | |
| Character Arc | Notes |

- Accountable
- Adaptable
- Adventurous
- Affable
- Alert
- Ambitious
- Appropriate
- Arrogant
- Assertive
- Astute
- Attentive
- Authentic
- Boorish
- Bossy
- Bravery
- Calm
- Candid
- Capable
- Charismatic
- Charming
- Collaborative
- Committed
- Communicator
- Compassionate
- Conceited
- Confident
- Connected
- Conscientious
- Considerate
- Consistent
- Cooperative
- Courageous
- Cowardly
- Creative
- Cultured
- Curious
- Dedicated
- Dependable
- Determined

- Diplomatic
- Disciplined
- Discreet
- Dishonest
- Dutiful
- Easygoing
- Efficient
- Empathetic
- Encouraging
- Energetic
- Enthusiastic
- Ethical
- Expressive
- Exuberant
- Facilitates
- Fair
- Fairness
- Faithful
- Fearless
- Finicky
- Flexible
- Friendly
- Generative
- Generosity
- Gratitude
- Gregarious
- Happy
- Hard-Working
- Helpful
- Honest
- Honorable
- Humble
- Humorous
- Imaginative
- Immaculate
- Impartial
- Impulsive
- Independent
- Inquiring

- Innovative
- Intelligent
- Intentional
- Interested
- Intimate
- Joyful
- Keen
- Knowledgeable
- Lazy
- Listener
- Lively
- Logical
- Loving
- Loyal
- Malicious
- Meticulous
- Networker
- Nurturing
- Obnoxious
- Observant
- Open-Minded
- Optimistic
- Organized
- Patient
- Peaceful
- Persistent
- Picky
- Planner
- Playful
- Poised
- Polite
- Pompous
- Powerful
- Pragmatic
- Precise
- Proactive
- Problem-Solver
- Productive
- Punctual

- Quarrelsome
- Reliable
- Resourceful
- Responsible
- Rude
- Sarcastic
- Self-centered
- Self-confident
- Self-reliant
- Sense of Humor
- Sensual
- Serves Others
- Sincere
- Skillful
- Slovenly
- Sneaky
- Spiritual
- Spontaneous
- Stable
- Stingy
- Strong
- Successful
- Sullen
- Supportive
- Surly
- Tactful
- Thoughtless
- Trusting
- Trusting
- Trustworthy
- Truthful
- Unfriendly
- Unruly
- Versatile
- Vibrant
- Vulgar
- Warm
- Wise
- Zealous

| Name/Nicknames | | Age/Birthday | Race |
|---|---|---|---|
| Height/Weight | Gender/Sexuality | Eyes | Hair color |
| Parents | | Place of Birth | Species |
| Siblings | | Class/Status | Education |
| Where they have lived | | Schools Attended | |
| Clothes/Glasses/Scars | | Spiritual Beliefs | |
| Occupation | | Awards/Accomplishments | |
| Strongest personality characteristics | | Favorite activities/Hobbies | |
| People they love | | People they hate | |
| People they admire | | Pets | Hobbies |
| Problems | | Dreams and Ambitions | |

| Important role in the story | |
|---|---|
| Past experiences that shaped who they are | |

| Character Arc | Notes |
|---|---|
| | |

- Accountable
- Adaptable
- Adventurous
- Affable
- Alert
- Ambitious
- Appropriate
- Arrogant
- Assertive
- Astute
- Attentive
- Authentic
- Boorish
- Bossy
- Bravery
- Calm
- Candid
- Capable
- Charismatic
- Charming
- Collaborative
- Committed
- Communicator
- Compassionate
- Conceited
- Confident
- Connected
- Conscientious
- Considerate
- Consistent
- Cooperative
- Courageous
- Cowardly
- Creative
- Cultured
- Curious
- Dedicated
- Dependable
- Determined
- Diplomatic
- Disciplined
- Discreet
- Dishonest
- Dutiful
- Easygoing
- Efficient
- Empathetic
- Encouraging
- Energetic
- Enthusiastic
- Ethical
- Expressive
- Exuberant
- Facilitates
- Fair
- Fairness
- Faithful
- Fearless
- Finicky
- Flexible
- Friendly
- Generative
- Generosity
- Gratitude
- Gregarious
- Happy
- Hard-Working
- Helpful
- Honest
- Honorable
- Humble
- Humorous
- Imaginative
- Immaculate
- Impartial
- Impulsive
- Independent
- Inquiring
- Innovative
- Intelligent
- Intentional
- Interested
- Intimate
- Joyful
- Keen
- Knowledgeable
- Lazy
- Listener
- Lively
- Logical
- Loving
- Loyal
- Malicious
- Meticulous
- Networker
- Nurturing
- Obnoxious
- Observant
- Open-Minded
- Optimistic
- Organized
- Patient
- Peaceful
- Persistent
- Picky
- Planner
- Playful
- Poised
- Polite
- Pompous
- Powerful
- Pragmatic
- Precise
- Proactive
- Problem-Solver
- Productive
- Punctual
- Quarrelsome
- Reliable
- Resourceful
- Responsible
- Rude
- Sarcastic
- Self-centered
- Self-confident
- Self-reliant
- Sense of Humor
- Sensual
- Serves Others
- Sincere
- Skillful
- Slovenly
- Sneaky
- Spiritual
- Spontaneous
- Stable
- Stingy
- Strong
- Successful
- Sullen
- Supportive
- Surly
- Tactful
- Thoughtless
- Trusting
- Trusting
- Trustworthy
- Truthful
- Unfriendly
- Unruly
- Versatile
- Vibrant
- Vulgar
- Warm
- Wise
- Zealous

| Name/Nicknames | | Age/Birthday | Race |
|---|---|---|---|
| Height/Weight | Gender/Sexuality | Eyes | Hair color |
| Parents | | Place of Birth | Species |
| Siblings | | Class/Status | Education |
| Where they have lived | | Schools Attended | |
| Clothes/Glasses/Scars | | Spiritual Beliefs | |
| Occupation | | Awards/Accomplishments | |
| Strongest personality characteristics | | Favorite activities/Hobbies | |
| People they love | | People they hate | |
| People they admire | | Pets | Hobbies |
| Problems | | Dreams and Ambitions | |

| Important role in the story | |
|---|---|
| Past experiences that shaped who they are | |
| Character Arc | Notes |

- Accountable
- Adaptable
- Adventurous
- Affable
- Alert
- Ambitious
- Appropriate
- Arrogant
- Assertive
- Astute
- Attentive
- Authentic
- Boorish
- Bossy
- Bravery
- Calm
- Candid
- Capable
- Charismatic
- Charming
- Collaborative
- Committed
- Communicator
- Compassionate
- Conceited
- Confident
- Connected
- Conscientious
- Considerate
- Consistent
- Cooperative
- Courageous
- Cowardly
- Creative
- Cultured
- Curious
- Dedicated
- Dependable
- Determined
- Diplomatic
- Disciplined
- Discreet
- Dishonest
- Dutiful
- Easygoing
- Efficient
- Empathetic
- Encouraging
- Energetic
- Enthusiastic
- Ethical
- Expressive
- Exuberant
- Facilitates
- Fair
- Fairness
- Faithful
- Fearless
- Finicky
- Flexible
- Friendly
- Generative
- Generosity
- Gratitude
- Gregarious
- Happy
- Hard-Working
- Helpful
- Honest
- Honorable
- Humble
- Humorous
- Imaginative
- Immaculate
- Impartial
- Impulsive
- Independent
- Inquiring
- Innovative
- Intelligent
- Intentional
- Interested
- Intimate
- Joyful
- Keen
- Knowledgeable
- Lazy
- Listener
- Lively
- Logical
- Loving
- Loyal
- Malicious
- Meticulous
- Networker
- Nurturing
- Obnoxious
- Observant
- Open-Minded
- Optimistic
- Organized
- Patient
- Peaceful
- Persistent
- Picky
- Planner
- Playful
- Poised
- Polite
- Pompous
- Powerful
- Pragmatic
- Precise
- Proactive
- Problem-Solver
- Productive
- Punctual
- Quarrelsome
- Reliable
- Resourceful
- Responsible
- Rude
- Sarcastic
- Self-centered
- Self-confident
- Self-reliant
- Sense of Humor
- Sensual
- Serves Others
- Sincere
- Skillful
- Slovenly
- Sneaky
- Spiritual
- Spontaneous
- Stable
- Stingy
- Strong
- Successful
- Sullen
- Supportive
- Surly
- Tactful
- Thoughtless
- Trusting
- Trusting
- Trustworthy
- Truthful
- Unfriendly
- Unruly
- Versatile
- Vibrant
- Vulgar
- Warm
- Wise
- Zealous

| Name/Nicknames | | Age/Birthday | Race |
|---|---|---|---|
| Height/Weight | Gender/Sexuality | Eyes | Hair color |
| Parents | | Place of Birth | Species |
| Siblings | | Class/Status | Education |
| Where they have lived | | Schools Attended | |
| Clothes/Glasses/Scars | | Spiritual Beliefs | |
| Occupation | | Awards/Accomplishments | |
| Strongest personality characteristics | | Favorite activities/Hobbies | |
| People they love | | People they hate | |
| People they admire | | Pets | Hobbies |
| Problems | | Dreams and Ambitions | |

| Important role in the story | |
|---|---|
| Past experiences that shaped who they are | |
| Character Arc | Notes |

| | | | | | | | |
|---|---|---|---|---|---|---|---|
| o | Accountable | o | Diplomatic | o | Innovative | o | Quarrelsome |
| o | Adaptable | o | Disciplined | o | Intelligent | o | Reliable |
| o | Adventurous | o | Discreet | o | Intentional | o | Resourceful |
| o | Affable | o | Dishonest | o | Interested | o | Responsible |
| o | Alert | o | Dutiful | o | Intimate | o | Rude |
| o | Ambitious | o | Easygoing | o | Joyful | o | Sarcastic |
| o | Appropriate | o | Efficient | o | Keen | o | Self-centered |
| o | Arrogant | o | Empathetic | o | Knowledgeable | o | Self-confident |
| o | Assertive | o | Encouraging | o | Lazy | o | Self-reliant |
| o | Astute | o | Energetic | o | Listener | o | Sense of Humor |
| o | Attentive | o | Enthusiastic | o | Lively | o | Sensual |
| o | Authentic | o | Ethical | o | Logical | o | Serves Others |
| o | Boorish | o | Expressive | o | Loving | o | Sincere |
| o | Bossy | o | Exuberant | o | Loyal | o | Skillful |
| o | Bravery | o | Facilitates | o | Malicious | o | Slovenly |
| o | Calm | o | Fair | o | Meticulous | o | Sneaky |
| o | Candid | o | Fairness | o | Networker | o | Spiritual |
| o | Capable | o | Faithful | o | Nurturing | o | Spontaneous |
| o | Charismatic | o | Fearless | o | Obnoxious | o | Stable |
| o | Charming | o | Finicky | o | Observant | o | Stingy |
| o | Collaborative | o | Flexible | o | Open-Minded | o | Strong |
| o | Committed | o | Friendly | o | Optimistic | o | Successful |
| o | Communicator | o | Generative | o | Organized | o | Sullen |
| o | Compassionate | o | Generosity | o | Patient | o | Supportive |
| o | Conceited | o | Gratitude | o | Peaceful | o | Surly |
| o | Confident | o | Gregarious | o | Persistent | o | Tactful |
| o | Connected | o | Happy | o | Picky | o | Thoughtless |
| o | Conscientious | o | Hard-Working | o | Planner | o | Trusting |
| o | Considerate | o | Helpful | o | Playful | o | Trusting |
| o | Consistent | o | Honest | o | Poised | o | Trustworthy |
| o | Cooperative | o | Honorable | o | Polite | o | Truthful |
| o | Courageous | o | Humble | o | Pompous | o | Unfriendly |
| o | Cowardly | o | Humorous | o | Powerful | o | Unruly |
| o | Creative | o | Imaginative | o | Pragmatic | o | Versatile |
| o | Cultured | o | Immaculate | o | Precise | o | Vibrant |
| o | Curious | o | Impartial | o | Proactive | o | Vulgar |
| o | Dedicated | o | Impulsive | o | Problem-Solver | o | Warm |
| o | Dependable | o | Independent | o | Productive | o | Wise |
| o | Determined | o | Inquiring | o | Punctual | o | Zealous |

| Name/Nicknames | | Age/Birthday | Race |
| --- | --- | --- | --- |
| Height/Weight | Gender/Sexuality | Eyes | Hair color |
| Parents | | Place of Birth | Species |
| Siblings | | Class/Status | Education |
| Where they have lived | | Schools Attended | |
| Clothes/Glasses/Scars | | Spiritual Beliefs | |
| Occupation | | Awards/Accomplishments | |
| Strongest personality characteristics | | Favorite activities/Hobbies | |
| People they love | | People they hate | |
| People they admire | | Pets | Hobbies |
| Problems | | Dreams and Ambitions | |

**Important role in the story**

**Past experiences that shaped who they are**

**Character Arc**

**Notes**

- Accountable
- Adaptable
- Adventurous
- Affable
- Alert
- Ambitious
- Appropriate
- Arrogant
- Assertive
- Astute
- Attentive
- Authentic
- Boorish
- Bossy
- Bravery
- Calm
- Candid
- Capable
- Charismatic
- Charming
- Collaborative
- Committed
- Communicator
- Compassionate
- Conceited
- Confident
- Connected
- Conscientious
- Considerate
- Consistent
- Cooperative
- Courageous
- Cowardly
- Creative
- Cultured
- Curious
- Dedicated
- Dependable
- Determined

- Diplomatic
- Disciplined
- Discreet
- Dishonest
- Dutiful
- Easygoing
- Efficient
- Empathetic
- Encouraging
- Energetic
- Enthusiastic
- Ethical
- Expressive
- Exuberant
- Facilitates
- Fair
- Fairness
- Faithful
- Fearless
- Finicky
- Flexible
- Friendly
- Generative
- Generosity
- Gratitude
- Gregarious
- Happy
- Hard-Working
- Helpful
- Honest
- Honorable
- Humble
- Humorous
- Imaginative
- Immaculate
- Impartial
- Impulsive
- Independent
- Inquiring

- Innovative
- Intelligent
- Intentional
- Interested
- Intimate
- Joyful
- Keen
- Knowledgeable
- Lazy
- Listener
- Lively
- Logical
- Loving
- Loyal
- Malicious
- Meticulous
- Networker
- Nurturing
- Obnoxious
- Observant
- Open-Minded
- Optimistic
- Organized
- Patient
- Peaceful
- Persistent
- Picky
- Planner
- Playful
- Poised
- Polite
- Pompous
- Powerful
- Pragmatic
- Precise
- Proactive
- Problem-Solver
- Productive
- Punctual

- Quarrelsome
- Reliable
- Resourceful
- Responsible
- Rude
- Sarcastic
- Self-centered
- Self-confident
- Self-reliant
- Sense of Humor
- Sensual
- Serves Others
- Sincere
- Skillful
- Slovenly
- Sneaky
- Spiritual
- Spontaneous
- Stable
- Stingy
- Strong
- Successful
- Sullen
- Supportive
- Surly
- Tactful
- Thoughtless
- Trusting
- Trusting
- Trustworthy
- Truthful
- Unfriendly
- Unruly
- Versatile
- Vibrant
- Vulgar
- Warm
- Wise
- Zealous

| Name/Nicknames | | Age/Birthday | Race |
|---|---|---|---|
| Height/Weight | Gender/Sexuality | Eyes | Hair color |
| Parents | | Place of Birth | Species |
| Siblings | | Class/Status | Education |
| Where they have lived | | Schools Attended | |
| Clothes/Glasses/Scars | | Spiritual Beliefs | |
| Occupation | | Awards/Accomplishments | |
| Strongest personality characteristics | | Favorite activities/Hobbies | |
| People they love | | People they hate | |
| People they admire | | Pets | Hobbies |
| Problems | | Dreams and Ambitions | |

| Important role in the story | |
|---|---|
| Past experiences that shaped who they are | |
| Character Arc | Notes |

| | | | | | | | |
|---|---|---|---|---|---|---|---|
| o | Accountable | o | Diplomatic | o | Innovative | o | Quarrelsome |
| o | Adaptable | o | Disciplined | o | Intelligent | o | Reliable |
| o | Adventurous | o | Discreet | o | Intentional | o | Resourceful |
| o | Affable | o | Dishonest | o | Interested | o | Responsible |
| o | Alert | o | Dutiful | o | Intimate | o | Rude |
| o | Ambitious | o | Easygoing | o | Joyful | o | Sarcastic |
| o | Appropriate | o | Efficient | o | Keen | o | Self-centered |
| o | Arrogant | o | Empathetic | o | Knowledgeable | o | Self-confident |
| o | Assertive | o | Encouraging | o | Lazy | o | Self-reliant |
| o | Astute | o | Energetic | o | Listener | o | Sense of Humor |
| o | Attentive | o | Enthusiastic | o | Lively | o | Sensual |
| o | Authentic | o | Ethical | o | Logical | o | Serves Others |
| o | Boorish | o | Expressive | o | Loving | o | Sincere |
| o | Bossy | o | Exuberant | o | Loyal | o | Skillful |
| o | Bravery | o | Facilitates | o | Malicious | o | Slovenly |
| o | Calm | o | Fair | o | Meticulous | o | Sneaky |
| o | Candid | o | Fairness | o | Networker | o | Spiritual |
| o | Capable | o | Faithful | o | Nurturing | o | Spontaneous |
| o | Charismatic | o | Fearless | o | Obnoxious | o | Stable |
| o | Charming | o | Finicky | o | Observant | o | Stingy |
| o | Collaborative | o | Flexible | o | Open-Minded | o | Strong |
| o | Committed | o | Friendly | o | Optimistic | o | Successful |
| o | Communicator | o | Generative | o | Organized | o | Sullen |
| o | Compassionate | o | Generosity | o | Patient | o | Supportive |
| o | Conceited | o | Gratitude | o | Peaceful | o | Surly |
| o | Confident | o | Gregarious | o | Persistent | o | Tactful |
| o | Connected | o | Happy | o | Picky | o | Thoughtless |
| o | Conscientious | o | Hard-Working | o | Planner | o | Trusting |
| o | Considerate | o | Helpful | o | Playful | o | Trusting |
| o | Consistent | o | Honest | o | Poised | o | Trustworthy |
| o | Cooperative | o | Honorable | o | Polite | o | Truthful |
| o | Courageous | o | Humble | o | Pompous | o | Unfriendly |
| o | Cowardly | o | Humorous | o | Powerful | o | Unruly |
| o | Creative | o | Imaginative | o | Pragmatic | o | Versatile |
| o | Cultured | o | Immaculate | o | Precise | o | Vibrant |
| o | Curious | o | Impartial | o | Proactive | o | Vulgar |
| o | Dedicated | o | Impulsive | o | Problem-Solver | o | Warm |
| o | Dependable | o | Independent | o | Productive | o | Wise |
| o | Determined | o | Inquiring | o | Punctual | o | Zealous |

| Name/Nicknames | | Age/Birthday | Race |
|---|---|---|---|
| Height/Weight | Gender/Sexuality | Eyes | Hair color |
| Parents | | Place of Birth | Species |
| Siblings | | Class/Status | Education |
| Where they have lived | | Schools Attended | |
| Clothes/Glasses/Scars | | Spiritual Beliefs | |
| Occupation | | Awards/Accomplishments | |
| Strongest personality characteristics | | Favorite activities/Hobbies | |
| People they love | | People they hate | |
| People they admire | | Pets | Hobbies |
| Problems | | Dreams and Ambitions | |

*Important role in the story*

*Past experiences that shaped who they are*

Character Arc

Notes

- Accountable
- Adaptable
- Adventurous
- Affable
- Alert
- Ambitious
- Appropriate
- Arrogant
- Assertive
- Astute
- Attentive
- Authentic
- Boorish
- Bossy
- Bravery
- Calm
- Candid
- Capable
- Charismatic
- Charming
- Collaborative
- Committed
- Communicator
- Compassionate
- Conceited
- Confident
- Connected
- Conscientious
- Considerate
- Consistent
- Cooperative
- Courageous
- Cowardly
- Creative
- Cultured
- Curious
- Dedicated
- Dependable
- Determined

- Diplomatic
- Disciplined
- Discreet
- Dishonest
- Dutiful
- Easygoing
- Efficient
- Empathetic
- Encouraging
- Energetic
- Enthusiastic
- Ethical
- Expressive
- Exuberant
- Facilitates
- Fair
- Fairness
- Faithful
- Fearless
- Finicky
- Flexible
- Friendly
- Generative
- Generosity
- Gratitude
- Gregarious
- Happy
- Hard-Working
- Helpful
- Honest
- Honorable
- Humble
- Humorous
- Imaginative
- Immaculate
- Impartial
- Impulsive
- Independent
- Inquiring

- Innovative
- Intelligent
- Intentional
- Interested
- Intimate
- Joyful
- Keen
- Knowledgeable
- Lazy
- Listener
- Lively
- Logical
- Loving
- Loyal
- Malicious
- Meticulous
- Networker
- Nurturing
- Obnoxious
- Observant
- Open-Minded
- Optimistic
- Organized
- Patient
- Peaceful
- Persistent
- Picky
- Planner
- Playful
- Poised
- Polite
- Pompous
- Powerful
- Pragmatic
- Precise
- Proactive
- Problem-Solver
- Productive
- Punctual

- Quarrelsome
- Reliable
- Resourceful
- Responsible
- Rude
- Sarcastic
- Self-centered
- Self-confident
- Self-reliant
- Sense of Humor
- Sensual
- Serves Others
- Sincere
- Skillful
- Slovenly
- Sneaky
- Spiritual
- Spontaneous
- Stable
- Stingy
- Strong
- Successful
- Sullen
- Supportive
- Surly
- Tactful
- Thoughtless
- Trusting
- Trusting
- Trustworthy
- Truthful
- Unfriendly
- Unruly
- Versatile
- Vibrant
- Vulgar
- Warm
- Wise
- Zealous

| Name/Nicknames | | Age/Birthday | Race |
|---|---|---|---|
| Height/Weight | Gender/Sexuality | Eyes | Hair color |
| Parents | | Place of Birth | Species |
| Siblings | | Class/Status | Education |
| Where they have lived | | Schools Attended | |
| Clothes/Glasses/Scars | | Spiritual Beliefs | |
| Occupation | | Awards/Accomplishments | |
| Strongest personality characteristics | | Favorite activities/Hobbies | |
| People they love | | People they hate | |
| People they admire | | Pets | Hobbies |
| Problems | | Dreams and Ambitions | |

| Important role in the story | |
|---|---|
| Past experiences that shaped who they are | |

| Character Arc | Notes |
|---|---|
| | |

| | | | | | | | |
|---|---|---|---|---|---|---|---|
| o | Accountable | o | Diplomatic | o | Innovative | o | Quarrelsome |
| o | Adaptable | o | Disciplined | o | Intelligent | o | Reliable |
| o | Adventurous | o | Discreet | o | Intentional | o | Resourceful |
| o | Affable | o | Dishonest | o | Interested | o | Responsible |
| o | Alert | o | Dutiful | o | Intimate | o | Rude |
| o | Ambitious | o | Easygoing | o | Joyful | o | Sarcastic |
| o | Appropriate | o | Efficient | o | Keen | o | Self-centered |
| o | Arrogant | o | Empathetic | o | Knowledgeable | o | Self-confident |
| o | Assertive | o | Encouraging | o | Lazy | o | Self-reliant |
| o | Astute | o | Energetic | o | Listener | o | Sense of Humor |
| o | Attentive | o | Enthusiastic | o | Lively | o | Sensual |
| o | Authentic | o | Ethical | o | Logical | o | Serves Others |
| o | Boorish | o | Expressive | o | Loving | o | Sincere |
| o | Bossy | o | Exuberant | o | Loyal | o | Skillful |
| o | Bravery | o | Facilitates | o | Malicious | o | Slovenly |
| o | Calm | o | Fair | o | Meticulous | o | Sneaky |
| o | Candid | o | Fairness | o | Networker | o | Spiritual |
| o | Capable | o | Faithful | o | Nurturing | o | Spontaneous |
| o | Charismatic | o | Fearless | o | Obnoxious | o | Stable |
| o | Charming | o | Finicky | o | Observant | o | Stingy |
| o | Collaborative | o | Flexible | o | Open-Minded | o | Strong |
| o | Committed | o | Friendly | o | Optimistic | o | Successful |
| o | Communicator | o | Generative | o | Organized | o | Sullen |
| o | Compassionate | o | Generosity | o | Patient | o | Supportive |
| o | Conceited | o | Gratitude | o | Peaceful | o | Surly |
| o | Confident | o | Gregarious | o | Persistent | o | Tactful |
| o | Connected | o | Happy | o | Picky | o | Thoughtless |
| o | Conscientious | o | Hard-Working | o | Planner | o | Trusting |
| o | Considerate | o | Helpful | o | Playful | o | Trusting |
| o | Consistent | o | Honest | o | Poised | o | Trustworthy |
| o | Cooperative | o | Honorable | o | Polite | o | Truthful |
| o | Courageous | o | Humble | o | Pompous | o | Unfriendly |
| o | Cowardly | o | Humorous | o | Powerful | o | Unruly |
| o | Creative | o | Imaginative | o | Pragmatic | o | Versatile |
| o | Cultured | o | Immaculate | o | Precise | o | Vibrant |
| o | Curious | o | Impartial | o | Proactive | o | Vulgar |
| o | Dedicated | o | Impulsive | o | Problem-Solver | o | Warm |
| o | Dependable | o | Independent | o | Productive | o | Wise |
| o | Determined | o | Inquiring | o | Punctual | o | Zealous |

| Name/Nicknames | | Age/Birthday | Race |
|---|---|---|---|
| Height/Weight | Gender/Sexuality | Eyes | Hair color |
| Parents | | Place of Birth | Species |
| Siblings | | Class/Status | Education |
| Where they have lived | | Schools Attended | |
| Clothes/Glasses/Scars | | Spiritual Beliefs | |
| Occupation | | Awards/Accomplishments | |
| Strongest personality characteristics | | Favorite activities/Hobbies | |
| People they love | | People they hate | |
| People they admire | | Pets | Hobbies |
| Problems | | Dreams and Ambitions | |

| | |
|---|---|
| *Important role in the story* | |
| *Past experiences that shaped who they are* | |

| Character Arc | Notes |
|---|---|
| | |

- ○ Accountable
- ○ Adaptable
- ○ Adventurous
- ○ Affable
- ○ Alert
- ○ Ambitious
- ○ Appropriate
- ○ Arrogant
- ○ Assertive
- ○ Astute
- ○ Attentive
- ○ Authentic
- ○ Boorish
- ○ Bossy
- ○ Bravery
- ○ Calm
- ○ Candid
- ○ Capable
- ○ Charismatic
- ○ Charming
- ○ Collaborative
- ○ Committed
- ○ Communicator
- ○ Compassionate
- ○ Conceited
- ○ Confident
- ○ Connected
- ○ Conscientious
- ○ Considerate
- ○ Consistent
- ○ Cooperative
- ○ Courageous
- ○ Cowardly
- ○ Creative
- ○ Cultured
- ○ Curious
- ○ Dedicated
- ○ Dependable
- ○ Determined

- ○ Diplomatic
- ○ Disciplined
- ○ Discreet
- ○ Dishonest
- ○ Dutiful
- ○ Easygoing
- ○ Efficient
- ○ Empathetic
- ○ Encouraging
- ○ Energetic
- ○ Enthusiastic
- ○ Ethical
- ○ Expressive
- ○ Exuberant
- ○ Facilitates
- ○ Fair
- ○ Fairness
- ○ Faithful
- ○ Fearless
- ○ Finicky
- ○ Flexible
- ○ Friendly
- ○ Generative
- ○ Generosity
- ○ Gratitude
- ○ Gregarious
- ○ Happy
- ○ Hard-Working
- ○ Helpful
- ○ Honest
- ○ Honorable
- ○ Humble
- ○ Humorous
- ○ Imaginative
- ○ Immaculate
- ○ Impartial
- ○ Impulsive
- ○ Independent
- ○ Inquiring

- ○ Innovative
- ○ Intelligent
- ○ Intentional
- ○ Interested
- ○ Intimate
- ○ Joyful
- ○ Keen
- ○ Knowledgeable
- ○ Lazy
- ○ Listener
- ○ Lively
- ○ Logical
- ○ Loving
- ○ Loyal
- ○ Malicious
- ○ Meticulous
- ○ Networker
- ○ Nurturing
- ○ Obnoxious
- ○ Observant
- ○ Open-Minded
- ○ Optimistic
- ○ Organized
- ○ Patient
- ○ Peaceful
- ○ Persistent
- ○ Picky
- ○ Planner
- ○ Playful
- ○ Poised
- ○ Polite
- ○ Pompous
- ○ Powerful
- ○ Pragmatic
- ○ Precise
- ○ Proactive
- ○ Problem-Solver
- ○ Productive
- ○ Punctual

- ○ Quarrelsome
- ○ Reliable
- ○ Resourceful
- ○ Responsible
- ○ Rude
- ○ Sarcastic
- ○ Self-centered
- ○ Self-confident
- ○ Self-reliant
- ○ Sense of Humor
- ○ Sensual
- ○ Serves Others
- ○ Sincere
- ○ Skillful
- ○ Slovenly
- ○ Sneaky
- ○ Spiritual
- ○ Spontaneous
- ○ Stable
- ○ Stingy
- ○ Strong
- ○ Successful
- ○ Sullen
- ○ Supportive
- ○ Surly
- ○ Tactful
- ○ Thoughtless
- ○ Trusting
- ○ Trusting
- ○ Trustworthy
- ○ Truthful
- ○ Unfriendly
- ○ Unruly
- ○ Versatile
- ○ Vibrant
- ○ Vulgar
- ○ Warm
- ○ Wise
- ○ Zealous

| Name/Nicknames | | Age/Birthday | Race |
|---|---|---|---|
| Height/Weight | Gender/Sexuality | Eyes | Hair color |
| Parents | | Place of Birth | Species |
| Siblings | | Class/Status | Education |
| Where they have lived | | Schools Attended | |
| Clothes/Glasses/Scars | | Spiritual Beliefs | |
| Occupation | | Awards/Accomplishments | |
| Strongest personality characteristics | | Favorite activities/Hobbies | |
| People they love | | People they hate | |
| People they admire | | Pets | Hobbies |
| Problems | | Dreams and Ambitions | |

| Important role in the story | |
|---|---|
| Past experiences that shaped who they are | |

| Character Arc | Notes |
|---|---|
|  |  |

| | | | |
|---|---|---|---|
| ○ Accountable | ○ Diplomatic | ○ Innovative | ○ Quarrelsome |
| ○ Adaptable | ○ Disciplined | ○ Intelligent | ○ Reliable |
| ○ Adventurous | ○ Discreet | ○ Intentional | ○ Resourceful |
| ○ Affable | ○ Dishonest | ○ Interested | ○ Responsible |
| ○ Alert | ○ Dutiful | ○ Intimate | ○ Rude |
| ○ Ambitious | ○ Easygoing | ○ Joyful | ○ Sarcastic |
| ○ Appropriate | ○ Efficient | ○ Keen | ○ Self-centered |
| ○ Arrogant | ○ Empathetic | ○ Knowledgeable | ○ Self-confident |
| ○ Assertive | ○ Encouraging | ○ Lazy | ○ Self-reliant |
| ○ Astute | ○ Energetic | ○ Listener | ○ Sense of Humor |
| ○ Attentive | ○ Enthusiastic | ○ Lively | ○ Sensual |
| ○ Authentic | ○ Ethical | ○ Logical | ○ Serves Others |
| ○ Boorish | ○ Expressive | ○ Loving | ○ Sincere |
| ○ Bossy | ○ Exuberant | ○ Loyal | ○ Skillful |
| ○ Bravery | ○ Facilitates | ○ Malicious | ○ Slovenly |
| ○ Calm | ○ Fair | ○ Meticulous | ○ Sneaky |
| ○ Candid | ○ Fairness | ○ Networker | ○ Spiritual |
| ○ Capable | ○ Faithful | ○ Nurturing | ○ Spontaneous |
| ○ Charismatic | ○ Fearless | ○ Obnoxious | ○ Stable |
| ○ Charming | ○ Finicky | ○ Observant | ○ Stingy |
| ○ Collaborative | ○ Flexible | ○ Open-Minded | ○ Strong |
| ○ Committed | ○ Friendly | ○ Optimistic | ○ Successful |
| ○ Communicator | ○ Generative | ○ Organized | ○ Sullen |
| ○ Compassionate | ○ Generosity | ○ Patient | ○ Supportive |
| ○ Conceited | ○ Gratitude | ○ Peaceful | ○ Surly |
| ○ Confident | ○ Gregarious | ○ Persistent | ○ Tactful |
| ○ Connected | ○ Happy | ○ Picky | ○ Thoughtless |
| ○ Conscientious | ○ Hard-Working | ○ Planner | ○ Trusting |
| ○ Considerate | ○ Helpful | ○ Playful | ○ Trusting |
| ○ Consistent | ○ Honest | ○ Poised | ○ Trustworthy |
| ○ Cooperative | ○ Honorable | ○ Polite | ○ Truthful |
| ○ Courageous | ○ Humble | ○ Pompous | ○ Unfriendly |
| ○ Cowardly | ○ Humorous | ○ Powerful | ○ Unruly |
| ○ Creative | ○ Imaginative | ○ Pragmatic | ○ Versatile |
| ○ Cultured | ○ Immaculate | ○ Precise | ○ Vibrant |
| ○ Curious | ○ Impartial | ○ Proactive | ○ Vulgar |
| ○ Dedicated | ○ Impulsive | ○ Problem-Solver | ○ Warm |
| ○ Dependable | ○ Independent | ○ Productive | ○ Wise |
| ○ Determined | ○ Inquiring | ○ Punctual | ○ Zealous |

| Name/Nicknames | | Age/Birthday | Race |
| --- | --- | --- | --- |
| Height/Weight | Gender/Sexuality | Eyes | Hair color |
| Parents | | Place of Birth | Species |
| Siblings | | Class/Status | Education |
| Where they have lived | | Schools Attended | |
| Clothes/Glasses/Scars | | Spiritual Beliefs | |
| Occupation | | Awards/Accomplishments | |
| Strongest personality characteristics | | Favorite activities/Hobbies | |
| People they love | | People they hate | |
| People they admire | | Pets | Hobbies |
| Problems | | Dreams and Ambitions | |

| Important role in the story | |
|---|---|
| Past experiences that shaped who they are | |

| Character Arc | Notes |
|---|---|
| | |

- Accountable
- Adaptable
- Adventurous
- Affable
- Alert
- Ambitious
- Appropriate
- Arrogant
- Assertive
- Astute
- Attentive
- Authentic
- Boorish
- Bossy
- Bravery
- Calm
- Candid
- Capable
- Charismatic
- Charming
- Collaborative
- Committed
- Communicator
- Compassionate
- Conceited
- Confident
- Connected
- Conscientious
- Considerate
- Consistent
- Cooperative
- Courageous
- Cowardly
- Creative
- Cultured
- Curious
- Dedicated
- Dependable
- Determined
- Diplomatic
- Disciplined
- Discreet
- Dishonest
- Dutiful
- Easygoing
- Efficient
- Empathetic
- Encouraging
- Energetic
- Enthusiastic
- Ethical
- Expressive
- Exuberant
- Facilitates
- Fair
- Fairness
- Faithful
- Fearless
- Finicky
- Flexible
- Friendly
- Generative
- Generosity
- Gratitude
- Gregarious
- Happy
- Hard-Working
- Helpful
- Honest
- Honorable
- Humble
- Humorous
- Imaginative
- Immaculate
- Impartial
- Impulsive
- Independent
- Inquiring
- Innovative
- Intelligent
- Intentional
- Interested
- Intimate
- Joyful
- Keen
- Knowledgeable
- Lazy
- Listener
- Lively
- Logical
- Loving
- Loyal
- Malicious
- Meticulous
- Networker
- Nurturing
- Obnoxious
- Observant
- Open-Minded
- Optimistic
- Organized
- Patient
- Peaceful
- Persistent
- Picky
- Planner
- Playful
- Poised
- Polite
- Pompous
- Powerful
- Pragmatic
- Precise
- Proactive
- Problem-Solver
- Productive
- Punctual
- Quarrelsome
- Reliable
- Resourceful
- Responsible
- Rude
- Sarcastic
- Self-centered
- Self-confident
- Self-reliant
- Sense of Humor
- Sensual
- Serves Others
- Sincere
- Skillful
- Slovenly
- Sneaky
- Spiritual
- Spontaneous
- Stable
- Stingy
- Strong
- Successful
- Sullen
- Supportive
- Surly
- Tactful
- Thoughtless
- Trusting
- Trusting
- Trustworthy
- Truthful
- Unfriendly
- Unruly
- Versatile
- Vibrant
- Vulgar
- Warm
- Wise
- Zealous

| Name/Nicknames | | Age/Birthday | Race |
|---|---|---|---|
| Height/Weight | Gender/Sexuality | Eyes | Hair color |
| Parents | | Place of Birth | Species |
| Siblings | | Class/Status | Education |
| Where they have lived | | Schools Attended | |
| Clothes/Glasses/Scars | | Spiritual Beliefs | |
| Occupation | | Awards/Accomplishments | |
| Strongest personality characteristics | | Favorite activities/Hobbies | |
| People they love | | People they hate | |
| People they admire | | Pets | Hobbies |
| Problems | | Dreams and Ambitions | |

| Important role in the story | |
|---|---|
| Past experiences that shaped who they are | |
| Character Arc | Notes |

- Accountable
- Adaptable
- Adventurous
- Affable
- Alert
- Ambitious
- Appropriate
- Arrogant
- Assertive
- Astute
- Attentive
- Authentic
- Boorish
- Bossy
- Bravery
- Calm
- Candid
- Capable
- Charismatic
- Charming
- Collaborative
- Committed
- Communicator
- Compassionate
- Conceited
- Confident
- Connected
- Conscientious
- Considerate
- Consistent
- Cooperative
- Courageous
- Cowardly
- Creative
- Cultured
- Curious
- Dedicated
- Dependable
- Determined
- Diplomatic
- Disciplined
- Discreet
- Dishonest
- Dutiful
- Easygoing
- Efficient
- Empathetic
- Encouraging
- Energetic
- Enthusiastic
- Ethical
- Expressive
- Exuberant
- Facilitates
- Fair
- Fairness
- Faithful
- Fearless
- Finicky
- Flexible
- Friendly
- Generative
- Generosity
- Gratitude
- Gregarious
- Happy
- Hard-Working
- Helpful
- Honest
- Honorable
- Humble
- Humorous
- Imaginative
- Immaculate
- Impartial
- Impulsive
- Independent
- Inquiring
- Innovative
- Intelligent
- Intentional
- Interested
- Intimate
- Joyful
- Keen
- Knowledgeable
- Lazy
- Listener
- Lively
- Logical
- Loving
- Loyal
- Malicious
- Meticulous
- Networker
- Nurturing
- Obnoxious
- Observant
- Open-Minded
- Optimistic
- Organized
- Patient
- Peaceful
- Persistent
- Picky
- Planner
- Playful
- Poised
- Polite
- Pompous
- Powerful
- Pragmatic
- Precise
- Proactive
- Problem-Solver
- Productive
- Punctual
- Quarrelsome
- Reliable
- Resourceful
- Responsible
- Rude
- Sarcastic
- Self-centered
- Self-confident
- Self-reliant
- Sense of Humor
- Sensual
- Serves Others
- Sincere
- Skillful
- Slovenly
- Sneaky
- Spiritual
- Spontaneous
- Stable
- Stingy
- Strong
- Successful
- Sullen
- Supportive
- Surly
- Tactful
- Thoughtless
- Trusting
- Trusting
- Trustworthy
- Truthful
- Unfriendly
- Unruly
- Versatile
- Vibrant
- Vulgar
- Warm
- Wise
- Zealous

| Name/Nicknames | | Age/Birthday | Race |
|---|---|---|---|
| Height/Weight | Gender/Sexuality | Eyes | Hair color |
| Parents | | Place of Birth | Species |
| Siblings | | Class/Status | Education |
| Where they have lived | | Schools Attended | |
| Clothes/Glasses/Scars | | Spiritual Beliefs | |
| Occupation | | Awards/Accomplishments | |
| Strongest personality characteristics | | Favorite activities/Hobbies | |
| People they love | | People they hate | |
| People they admire | | Pets | Hobbies |
| Problems | | Dreams and Ambitions | |

| Important role in the story | |
|---|---|
| Past experiences that shaped who they are | |

| Character Arc | Notes |
|---|---|

| | | | | | | | |
|---|---|---|---|---|---|---|---|
| o | Accountable | o | Diplomatic | o | Innovative | o | Quarrelsome |
| o | Adaptable | o | Disciplined | o | Intelligent | o | Reliable |
| o | Adventurous | o | Discreet | o | Intentional | o | Resourceful |
| o | Affable | o | Dishonest | o | Interested | o | Responsible |
| o | Alert | o | Dutiful | o | Intimate | o | Rude |
| o | Ambitious | o | Easygoing | o | Joyful | o | Sarcastic |
| o | Appropriate | o | Efficient | o | Keen | o | Self-centered |
| o | Arrogant | o | Empathetic | o | Knowledgeable | o | Self-confident |
| o | Assertive | o | Encouraging | o | Lazy | o | Self-reliant |
| o | Astute | o | Energetic | o | Listener | o | Sense of Humor |
| o | Attentive | o | Enthusiastic | o | Lively | o | Sensual |
| o | Authentic | o | Ethical | o | Logical | o | Serves Others |
| o | Boorish | o | Expressive | o | Loving | o | Sincere |
| o | Bossy | o | Exuberant | o | Loyal | o | Skillful |
| o | Bravery | o | Facilitates | o | Malicious | o | Slovenly |
| o | Calm | o | Fair | o | Meticulous | o | Sneaky |
| o | Candid | o | Fairness | o | Networker | o | Spiritual |
| o | Capable | o | Faithful | o | Nurturing | o | Spontaneous |
| o | Charismatic | o | Fearless | o | Obnoxious | o | Stable |
| o | Charming | o | Finicky | o | Observant | o | Stingy |
| o | Collaborative | o | Flexible | o | Open-Minded | o | Strong |
| o | Committed | o | Friendly | o | Optimistic | o | Successful |
| o | Communicator | o | Generative | o | Organized | o | Sullen |
| o | Compassionate | o | Generosity | o | Patient | o | Supportive |
| o | Conceited | o | Gratitude | o | Peaceful | o | Surly |
| o | Confident | o | Gregarious | o | Persistent | o | Tactful |
| o | Connected | o | Happy | o | Picky | o | Thoughtless |
| o | Conscientious | o | Hard-Working | o | Planner | o | Trusting |
| o | Considerate | o | Helpful | o | Playful | o | Trusting |
| o | Consistent | o | Honest | o | Poised | o | Trustworthy |
| o | Cooperative | o | Honorable | o | Polite | o | Truthful |
| o | Courageous | o | Humble | o | Pompous | o | Unfriendly |
| o | Cowardly | o | Humorous | o | Powerful | o | Unruly |
| o | Creative | o | Imaginative | o | Pragmatic | o | Versatile |
| o | Cultured | o | Immaculate | o | Precise | o | Vibrant |
| o | Curious | o | Impartial | o | Proactive | o | Vulgar |
| o | Dedicated | o | Impulsive | o | Problem-Solver | o | Warm |
| o | Dependable | o | Independent | o | Productive | o | Wise |
| o | Determined | o | Inquiring | o | Punctual | o | Zealous |

| Name/Nicknames | | Age/Birthday | Race |
| --- | --- | --- | --- |
| Height/Weight | Gender/Sexuality | Eyes | Hair color |
| Parents | | Place of Birth | Species |
| Siblings | | Class/Status | Education |
| Where they have lived | | Schools Attended | |
| Clothes/Glasses/Scars | | Spiritual Beliefs | |
| Occupation | | Awards/Accomplishments | |
| Strongest personality characteristics | | Favorite activities/Hobbies | |
| People they love | | People they hate | |
| People they admire | | Pets | Hobbies |
| Problems | | Dreams and Ambitions | |

| | |
|---|---|
| *Important role in the story* | |
| *Past experiences that shaped who they are* | |

| Character Arc | Notes |
|---|---|
| | |

- ○ Accountable
- ○ Adaptable
- ○ Adventurous
- ○ Affable
- ○ Alert
- ○ Ambitious
- ○ Appropriate
- ○ Arrogant
- ○ Assertive
- ○ Astute
- ○ Attentive
- ○ Authentic
- ○ Boorish
- ○ Bossy
- ○ Bravery
- ○ Calm
- ○ Candid
- ○ Capable
- ○ Charismatic
- ○ Charming
- ○ Collaborative
- ○ Committed
- ○ Communicator
- ○ Compassionate
- ○ Conceited
- ○ Confident
- ○ Connected
- ○ Conscientious
- ○ Considerate
- ○ Consistent
- ○ Cooperative
- ○ Courageous
- ○ Cowardly
- ○ Creative
- ○ Cultured
- ○ Curious
- ○ Dedicated
- ○ Dependable
- ○ Determined

- ○ Diplomatic
- ○ Disciplined
- ○ Discreet
- ○ Dishonest
- ○ Dutiful
- ○ Easygoing
- ○ Efficient
- ○ Empathetic
- ○ Encouraging
- ○ Energetic
- ○ Enthusiastic
- ○ Ethical
- ○ Expressive
- ○ Exuberant
- ○ Facilitates
- ○ Fair
- ○ Fairness
- ○ Faithful
- ○ Fearless
- ○ Finicky
- ○ Flexible
- ○ Friendly
- ○ Generative
- ○ Generosity
- ○ Gratitude
- ○ Gregarious
- ○ Happy
- ○ Hard-Working
- ○ Helpful
- ○ Honest
- ○ Honorable
- ○ Humble
- ○ Humorous
- ○ Imaginative
- ○ Immaculate
- ○ Impartial
- ○ Impulsive
- ○ Independent
- ○ Inquiring

- ○ Innovative
- ○ Intelligent
- ○ Intentional
- ○ Interested
- ○ Intimate
- ○ Joyful
- ○ Keen
- ○ Knowledgeable
- ○ Lazy
- ○ Listener
- ○ Lively
- ○ Logical
- ○ Loving
- ○ Loyal
- ○ Malicious
- ○ Meticulous
- ○ Networker
- ○ Nurturing
- ○ Obnoxious
- ○ Observant
- ○ Open-Minded
- ○ Optimistic
- ○ Organized
- ○ Patient
- ○ Peaceful
- ○ Persistent
- ○ Picky
- ○ Planner
- ○ Playful
- ○ Poised
- ○ Polite
- ○ Pompous
- ○ Powerful
- ○ Pragmatic
- ○ Precise
- ○ Proactive
- ○ Problem-Solver
- ○ Productive
- ○ Punctual

- ○ Quarrelsome
- ○ Reliable
- ○ Resourceful
- ○ Responsible
- ○ Rude
- ○ Sarcastic
- ○ Self-centered
- ○ Self-confident
- ○ Self-reliant
- ○ Sense of Humor
- ○ Sensual
- ○ Serves Others
- ○ Sincere
- ○ Skillful
- ○ Slovenly
- ○ Sneaky
- ○ Spiritual
- ○ Spontaneous
- ○ Stable
- ○ Stingy
- ○ Strong
- ○ Successful
- ○ Sullen
- ○ Supportive
- ○ Surly
- ○ Tactful
- ○ Thoughtless
- ○ Trusting
- ○ Trusting
- ○ Trustworthy
- ○ Truthful
- ○ Unfriendly
- ○ Unruly
- ○ Versatile
- ○ Vibrant
- ○ Vulgar
- ○ Warm
- ○ Wise
- ○ Zealous

| Name/Nicknames | | Age/Birthday | Race |
| --- | --- | --- | --- |
| Height/Weight | Gender/Sexuality | Eyes | Hair color |
| Parents | | Place of Birth | Species |
| Siblings | | Class/Status | Education |
| Where they have lived | | Schools Attended | |
| Clothes/Glasses/Scars | | Spiritual Beliefs | |
| Occupation | | Awards/Accomplishments | |
| Strongest personality characteristics | | Favorite activities/Hobbies | |
| People they love | | People they hate | |
| People they admire | | Pets | Hobbies |
| Problems | | Dreams and Ambitions | |

| | |
|---|---|
| *Important role in the story* | |
| *Past experiences that shaped who they are* | |

| Character Arc | Notes |
|---|---|
| | |

- Accountable
- Adaptable
- Adventurous
- Affable
- Alert
- Ambitious
- Appropriate
- Arrogant
- Assertive
- Astute
- Attentive
- Authentic
- Boorish
- Bossy
- Bravery
- Calm
- Candid
- Capable
- Charismatic
- Charming
- Collaborative
- Committed
- Communicator
- Compassionate
- Conceited
- Confident
- Connected
- Conscientious
- Considerate
- Consistent
- Cooperative
- Courageous
- Cowardly
- Creative
- Cultured
- Curious
- Dedicated
- Dependable
- Determined
- Diplomatic
- Disciplined
- Discreet
- Dishonest
- Dutiful
- Easygoing
- Efficient
- Empathetic
- Encouraging
- Energetic
- Enthusiastic
- Ethical
- Expressive
- Exuberant
- Facilitates
- Fair
- Fairness
- Faithful
- Fearless
- Finicky
- Flexible
- Friendly
- Generative
- Generosity
- Gratitude
- Gregarious
- Happy
- Hard-Working
- Helpful
- Honest
- Honorable
- Humble
- Humorous
- Imaginative
- Immaculate
- Impartial
- Impulsive
- Independent
- Inquiring
- Innovative
- Intelligent
- Intentional
- Interested
- Intimate
- Joyful
- Keen
- Knowledgeable
- Lazy
- Listener
- Lively
- Logical
- Loving
- Loyal
- Malicious
- Meticulous
- Networker
- Nurturing
- Obnoxious
- Observant
- Open-Minded
- Optimistic
- Organized
- Patient
- Peaceful
- Persistent
- Picky
- Planner
- Playful
- Poised
- Polite
- Pompous
- Powerful
- Pragmatic
- Precise
- Proactive
- Problem-Solver
- Productive
- Punctual
- Quarrelsome
- Reliable
- Resourceful
- Responsible
- Rude
- Sarcastic
- Self-centered
- Self-confident
- Self-reliant
- Sense of Humor
- Sensual
- Serves Others
- Sincere
- Skillful
- Slovenly
- Sneaky
- Spiritual
- Spontaneous
- Stable
- Stingy
- Strong
- Successful
- Sullen
- Supportive
- Surly
- Tactful
- Thoughtless
- Trusting
- Trusting
- Trustworthy
- Truthful
- Unfriendly
- Unruly
- Versatile
- Vibrant
- Vulgar
- Warm
- Wise
- Zealous

| Name/Nicknames | | Age/Birthday | Race |
|---|---|---|---|
| Height/Weight | Gender/Sexuality | Eyes | Hair color |
| Parents | | Place of Birth | Species |
| Siblings | | Class/Status | Education |
| Where they have lived | | Schools Attended | |
| Clothes/Glasses/Scars | | Spiritual Beliefs | |
| Occupation | | Awards/Accomplishments | |
| Strongest personality characteristics | | Favorite activities/Hobbies | |
| People they love | | People they hate | |
| People they admire | | Pets | Hobbies |
| Problems | | Dreams and Ambitions | |

| Important role in the story | |
|---|---|
| Past experiences that shaped who they are | |

| Character Arc | Notes |
|---|---|
| | |

| | | | | | | | |
|---|---|---|---|---|---|---|---|
| o | Accountable | o | Diplomatic | o | Innovative | o | Quarrelsome |
| o | Adaptable | o | Disciplined | o | Intelligent | o | Reliable |
| o | Adventurous | o | Discreet | o | Intentional | o | Resourceful |
| o | Affable | o | Dishonest | o | Interested | o | Responsible |
| o | Alert | o | Dutiful | o | Intimate | o | Rude |
| o | Ambitious | o | Easygoing | o | Joyful | o | Sarcastic |
| o | Appropriate | o | Efficient | o | Keen | o | Self-centered |
| o | Arrogant | o | Empathetic | o | Knowledgeable | o | Self-confident |
| o | Assertive | o | Encouraging | o | Lazy | o | Self-reliant |
| o | Astute | o | Energetic | o | Listener | o | Sense of Humor |
| o | Attentive | o | Enthusiastic | o | Lively | o | Sensual |
| o | Authentic | o | Ethical | o | Logical | o | Serves Others |
| o | Boorish | o | Expressive | o | Loving | o | Sincere |
| o | Bossy | o | Exuberant | o | Loyal | o | Skillful |
| o | Bravery | o | Facilitates | o | Malicious | o | Slovenly |
| o | Calm | o | Fair | o | Meticulous | o | Sneaky |
| o | Candid | o | Fairness | o | Networker | o | Spiritual |
| o | Capable | o | Faithful | o | Nurturing | o | Spontaneous |
| o | Charismatic | o | Fearless | o | Obnoxious | o | Stable |
| o | Charming | o | Finicky | o | Observant | o | Stingy |
| o | Collaborative | o | Flexible | o | Open-Minded | o | Strong |
| o | Committed | o | Friendly | o | Optimistic | o | Successful |
| o | Communicator | o | Generative | o | Organized | o | Sullen |
| o | Compassionate | o | Generosity | o | Patient | o | Supportive |
| o | Conceited | o | Gratitude | o | Peaceful | o | Surly |
| o | Confident | o | Gregarious | o | Persistent | o | Tactful |
| o | Connected | o | Happy | o | Picky | o | Thoughtless |
| o | Conscientious | o | Hard-Working | o | Planner | o | Trusting |
| o | Considerate | o | Helpful | o | Playful | o | Trusting |
| o | Consistent | o | Honest | o | Poised | o | Trustworthy |
| o | Cooperative | o | Honorable | o | Polite | o | Truthful |
| o | Courageous | o | Humble | o | Pompous | o | Unfriendly |
| o | Cowardly | o | Humorous | o | Powerful | o | Unruly |
| o | Creative | o | Imaginative | o | Pragmatic | o | Versatile |
| o | Cultured | o | Immaculate | o | Precise | o | Vibrant |
| o | Curious | o | Impartial | o | Proactive | o | Vulgar |
| o | Dedicated | o | Impulsive | o | Problem-Solver | o | Warm |
| o | Dependable | o | Independent | o | Productive | o | Wise |
| o | Determined | o | Inquiring | o | Punctual | o | Zealous |

| Name/Nicknames | | Age/Birthday | Race |
| --- | --- | --- | --- |
| Height/Weight | Gender/Sexuality | Eyes | Hair color |
| Parents | | Place of Birth | Species |
| Siblings | | Class/Status | Education |
| Where they have lived | | Schools Attended | |
| Clothes/Glasses/Scars | | Spiritual Beliefs | |
| Occupation | | Awards/Accomplishments | |
| Strongest personality characteristics | | Favorite activities/Hobbies | |
| People they love | | People they hate | |
| People they admire | | Pets | Hobbies |
| Problems | | Dreams and Ambitions | |

*Important role in the story*

*Past experiences that shaped who they are*

*Character Arc*

*Notes*

- Accountable
- Adaptable
- Adventurous
- Affable
- Alert
- Ambitious
- Appropriate
- Arrogant
- Assertive
- Astute
- Attentive
- Authentic
- Boorish
- Bossy
- Bravery
- Calm
- Candid
- Capable
- Charismatic
- Charming
- Collaborative
- Committed
- Communicator
- Compassionate
- Conceited
- Confident
- Connected
- Conscientious
- Considerate
- Consistent
- Cooperative
- Courageous
- Cowardly
- Creative
- Cultured
- Curious
- Dedicated
- Dependable
- Determined
- Diplomatic
- Disciplined
- Discreet
- Dishonest
- Dutiful
- Easygoing
- Efficient
- Empathetic
- Encouraging
- Energetic
- Enthusiastic
- Ethical
- Expressive
- Exuberant
- Facilitates
- Fair
- Fairness
- Faithful
- Fearless
- Finicky
- Flexible
- Friendly
- Generative
- Generosity
- Gratitude
- Gregarious
- Happy
- Hard-Working
- Helpful
- Honest
- Honorable
- Humble
- Humorous
- Imaginative
- Immaculate
- Impartial
- Impulsive
- Independent
- Inquiring
- Innovative
- Intelligent
- Intentional
- Interested
- Intimate
- Joyful
- Keen
- Knowledgeable
- Lazy
- Listener
- Lively
- Logical
- Loving
- Loyal
- Malicious
- Meticulous
- Networker
- Nurturing
- Obnoxious
- Observant
- Open-Minded
- Optimistic
- Organized
- Patient
- Peaceful
- Persistent
- Picky
- Planner
- Playful
- Poised
- Polite
- Pompous
- Powerful
- Pragmatic
- Precise
- Proactive
- Problem-Solver
- Productive
- Punctual
- Quarrelsome
- Reliable
- Resourceful
- Responsible
- Rude
- Sarcastic
- Self-centered
- Self-confident
- Self-reliant
- Sense of Humor
- Sensual
- Serves Others
- Sincere
- Skillful
- Slovenly
- Sneaky
- Spiritual
- Spontaneous
- Stable
- Stingy
- Strong
- Successful
- Sullen
- Supportive
- Surly
- Tactful
- Thoughtless
- Trusting
- Trusting
- Trustworthy
- Truthful
- Unfriendly
- Unruly
- Versatile
- Vibrant
- Vulgar
- Warm
- Wise
- Zealous

| Name/Nicknames | | Age/Birthday | Race |
|---|---|---|---|
| Height/Weight | Gender/Sexuality | Eyes | Hair color |
| Parents | | Place of Birth | Species |
| Siblings | | Class/Status | Education |
| Where they have lived | | Schools Attended | |
| Clothes/Glasses/Scars | | Spiritual Beliefs | |
| Occupation | | Awards/Accomplishments | |
| Strongest personality characteristics | | Favorite activities/Hobbies | |
| People they love | | People they hate | |
| People they admire | | Pets | Hobbies |
| Problems | | Dreams and Ambitions | |

| Important role in the story | |
|---|---|
| Past experiences that shaped who they are | |

| Character Arc | Notes |
|---|---|
| | |

- Accountable
- Adaptable
- Adventurous
- Affable
- Alert
- Ambitious
- Appropriate
- Arrogant
- Assertive
- Astute
- Attentive
- Authentic
- Boorish
- Bossy
- Bravery
- Calm
- Candid
- Capable
- Charismatic
- Charming
- Collaborative
- Committed
- Communicator
- Compassionate
- Conceited
- Confident
- Connected
- Conscientious
- Considerate
- Consistent
- Cooperative
- Courageous
- Cowardly
- Creative
- Cultured
- Curious
- Dedicated
- Dependable
- Determined

- Diplomatic
- Disciplined
- Discreet
- Dishonest
- Dutiful
- Easygoing
- Efficient
- Empathetic
- Encouraging
- Energetic
- Enthusiastic
- Ethical
- Expressive
- Exuberant
- Facilitates
- Fair
- Fairness
- Faithful
- Fearless
- Finicky
- Flexible
- Friendly
- Generative
- Generosity
- Gratitude
- Gregarious
- Happy
- Hard-Working
- Helpful
- Honest
- Honorable
- Humble
- Humorous
- Imaginative
- Immaculate
- Impartial
- Impulsive
- Independent
- Inquiring

- Innovative
- Intelligent
- Intentional
- Interested
- Intimate
- Joyful
- Keen
- Knowledgeable
- Lazy
- Listener
- Lively
- Logical
- Loving
- Loyal
- Malicious
- Meticulous
- Networker
- Nurturing
- Obnoxious
- Observant
- Open-Minded
- Optimistic
- Organized
- Patient
- Peaceful
- Persistent
- Picky
- Planner
- Playful
- Poised
- Polite
- Pompous
- Powerful
- Pragmatic
- Precise
- Proactive
- Problem-Solver
- Productive
- Punctual

- Quarrelsome
- Reliable
- Resourceful
- Responsible
- Rude
- Sarcastic
- Self-centered
- Self-confident
- Self-reliant
- Sense of Humor
- Sensual
- Serves Others
- Sincere
- Skillful
- Slovenly
- Sneaky
- Spiritual
- Spontaneous
- Stable
- Stingy
- Strong
- Successful
- Sullen
- Supportive
- Surly
- Tactful
- Thoughtless
- Trusting
- Trusting
- Trustworthy
- Truthful
- Unfriendly
- Unruly
- Versatile
- Vibrant
- Vulgar
- Warm
- Wise
- Zealous

| Name/Nicknames | | Age/Birthday | Race |
| --- | --- | --- | --- |
| Height/Weight | Gender/Sexuality | Eyes | Hair color |
| Parents | | Place of Birth | Species |
| Siblings | | Class/Status | Education |
| Where they have lived | | Schools Attended | |
| Clothes/Glasses/Scars | | Spiritual Beliefs | |
| Occupation | | Awards/Accomplishments | |
| Strongest personality characteristics | | Favorite activities/Hobbies | |
| People they love | | People they hate | |
| People they admire | | Pets | Hobbies |
| Problems | | Dreams and Ambitions | |

| | |
|---|---|
| *Important role in the story* | |
| *Past experiences that shaped who they are* | |

| Character Arc | Notes |
|---|---|
| | |

- ○ Accountable
- ○ Adaptable
- ○ Adventurous
- ○ Affable
- ○ Alert
- ○ Ambitious
- ○ Appropriate
- ○ Arrogant
- ○ Assertive
- ○ Astute
- ○ Attentive
- ○ Authentic
- ○ Boorish
- ○ Bossy
- ○ Bravery
- ○ Calm
- ○ Candid
- ○ Capable
- ○ Charismatic
- ○ Charming
- ○ Collaborative
- ○ Committed
- ○ Communicator
- ○ Compassionate
- ○ Conceited
- ○ Confident
- ○ Connected
- ○ Conscientious
- ○ Considerate
- ○ Consistent
- ○ Cooperative
- ○ Courageous
- ○ Cowardly
- ○ Creative
- ○ Cultured
- ○ Curious
- ○ Dedicated
- ○ Dependable
- ○ Determined
- ○ Diplomatic
- ○ Disciplined
- ○ Discreet
- ○ Dishonest
- ○ Dutiful
- ○ Easygoing
- ○ Efficient
- ○ Empathetic
- ○ Encouraging
- ○ Energetic
- ○ Enthusiastic
- ○ Ethical
- ○ Expressive
- ○ Exuberant
- ○ Facilitates
- ○ Fair
- ○ Fairness
- ○ Faithful
- ○ Fearless
- ○ Finicky
- ○ Flexible
- ○ Friendly
- ○ Generative
- ○ Generosity
- ○ Gratitude
- ○ Gregarious
- ○ Happy
- ○ Hard-Working
- ○ Helpful
- ○ Honest
- ○ Honorable
- ○ Humble
- ○ Humorous
- ○ Imaginative
- ○ Immaculate
- ○ Impartial
- ○ Impulsive
- ○ Independent
- ○ Inquiring
- ○ Innovative
- ○ Intelligent
- ○ Intentional
- ○ Interested
- ○ Intimate
- ○ Joyful
- ○ Keen
- ○ Knowledgeable
- ○ Lazy
- ○ Listener
- ○ Lively
- ○ Logical
- ○ Loving
- ○ Loyal
- ○ Malicious
- ○ Meticulous
- ○ Networker
- ○ Nurturing
- ○ Obnoxious
- ○ Observant
- ○ Open-Minded
- ○ Optimistic
- ○ Organized
- ○ Patient
- ○ Peaceful
- ○ Persistent
- ○ Picky
- ○ Planner
- ○ Playful
- ○ Poised
- ○ Polite
- ○ Pompous
- ○ Powerful
- ○ Pragmatic
- ○ Precise
- ○ Proactive
- ○ Problem-Solver
- ○ Productive
- ○ Punctual
- ○ Quarrelsome
- ○ Reliable
- ○ Resourceful
- ○ Responsible
- ○ Rude
- ○ Sarcastic
- ○ Self-centered
- ○ Self-confident
- ○ Self-reliant
- ○ Sense of Humor
- ○ Sensual
- ○ Serves Others
- ○ Sincere
- ○ Skillful
- ○ Slovenly
- ○ Sneaky
- ○ Spiritual
- ○ Spontaneous
- ○ Stable
- ○ Stingy
- ○ Strong
- ○ Successful
- ○ Sullen
- ○ Supportive
- ○ Surly
- ○ Tactful
- ○ Thoughtless
- ○ Trusting
- ○ Trusting
- ○ Trustworthy
- ○ Truthful
- ○ Unfriendly
- ○ Unruly
- ○ Versatile
- ○ Vibrant
- ○ Vulgar
- ○ Warm
- ○ Wise
- ○ Zealous

| Name/Nicknames | | Age/Birthday | Race |
|---|---|---|---|
| Height/Weight | Gender/Sexuality | Eyes | Hair color |
| Parents | | Place of Birth | Species |
| Siblings | | Class/Status | Education |
| Where they have lived | | Schools Attended | |
| Clothes/Glasses/Scars | | Spiritual Beliefs | |
| Occupation | | Awards/Accomplishments | |
| Strongest personality characteristics | | Favorite activities/Hobbies | |
| People they love | | People they hate | |
| People they admire | | Pets | Hobbies |
| Problems | | Dreams and Ambitions | |

| Important role in the story | |
|---|---|
| Past experiences that shaped who they are | |

| Character Arc | Notes |
|---|---|
| | |

| | | | | | | | |
|---|---|---|---|---|---|---|---|
| ○ | Accountable | ○ | Diplomatic | ○ | Innovative | ○ | Quarrelsome |
| ○ | Adaptable | ○ | Disciplined | ○ | Intelligent | ○ | Reliable |
| ○ | Adventurous | ○ | Discreet | ○ | Intentional | ○ | Resourceful |
| ○ | Affable | ○ | Dishonest | ○ | Interested | ○ | Responsible |
| ○ | Alert | ○ | Dutiful | ○ | Intimate | ○ | Rude |
| ○ | Ambitious | ○ | Easygoing | ○ | Joyful | ○ | Sarcastic |
| ○ | Appropriate | ○ | Efficient | ○ | Keen | ○ | Self-centered |
| ○ | Arrogant | ○ | Empathetic | ○ | Knowledgeable | ○ | Self-confident |
| ○ | Assertive | ○ | Encouraging | ○ | Lazy | ○ | Self-reliant |
| ○ | Astute | ○ | Energetic | ○ | Listener | ○ | Sense of Humor |
| ○ | Attentive | ○ | Enthusiastic | ○ | Lively | ○ | Sensual |
| ○ | Authentic | ○ | Ethical | ○ | Logical | ○ | Serves Others |
| ○ | Boorish | ○ | Expressive | ○ | Loving | ○ | Sincere |
| ○ | Bossy | ○ | Exuberant | ○ | Loyal | ○ | Skillful |
| ○ | Bravery | ○ | Facilitates | ○ | Malicious | ○ | Slovenly |
| ○ | Calm | ○ | Fair | ○ | Meticulous | ○ | Sneaky |
| ○ | Candid | ○ | Fairness | ○ | Networker | ○ | Spiritual |
| ○ | Capable | ○ | Faithful | ○ | Nurturing | ○ | Spontaneous |
| ○ | Charismatic | ○ | Fearless | ○ | Obnoxious | ○ | Stable |
| ○ | Charming | ○ | Finicky | ○ | Observant | ○ | Stingy |
| ○ | Collaborative | ○ | Flexible | ○ | Open-Minded | ○ | Strong |
| ○ | Committed | ○ | Friendly | ○ | Optimistic | ○ | Successful |
| ○ | Communicator | ○ | Generative | ○ | Organized | ○ | Sullen |
| ○ | Compassionate | ○ | Generosity | ○ | Patient | ○ | Supportive |
| ○ | Conceited | ○ | Gratitude | ○ | Peaceful | ○ | Surly |
| ○ | Confident | ○ | Gregarious | ○ | Persistent | ○ | Tactful |
| ○ | Connected | ○ | Happy | ○ | Picky | ○ | Thoughtless |
| ○ | Conscientious | ○ | Hard-Working | ○ | Planner | ○ | Trusting |
| ○ | Considerate | ○ | Helpful | ○ | Playful | ○ | Trusting |
| ○ | Consistent | ○ | Honest | ○ | Poised | ○ | Trustworthy |
| ○ | Cooperative | ○ | Honorable | ○ | Polite | ○ | Truthful |
| ○ | Courageous | ○ | Humble | ○ | Pompous | ○ | Unfriendly |
| ○ | Cowardly | ○ | Humorous | ○ | Powerful | ○ | Unruly |
| ○ | Creative | ○ | Imaginative | ○ | Pragmatic | ○ | Versatile |
| ○ | Cultured | ○ | Immaculate | ○ | Precise | ○ | Vibrant |
| ○ | Curious | ○ | Impartial | ○ | Proactive | ○ | Vulgar |
| ○ | Dedicated | ○ | Impulsive | ○ | Problem-Solver | ○ | Warm |
| ○ | Dependable | ○ | Independent | ○ | Productive | ○ | Wise |
| ○ | Determined | ○ | Inquiring | ○ | Punctual | ○ | Zealous |

| Name/Nicknames | | Age/Birthday | Race |
|---|---|---|---|
| Height/Weight | Gender/Sexuality | Eyes | Hair color |
| Parents | | Place of Birth | Species |
| Siblings | | Class/Status | Education |
| Where they have lived | | Schools Attended | |
| Clothes/Glasses/Scars | | Spiritual Beliefs | |
| Occupation | | Awards/Accomplishments | |
| Strongest personality characteristics | | Favorite activities/Hobbies | |
| People they love | | People they hate | |
| People they admire | | Pets | Hobbies |
| Problems | | Dreams and Ambitions | |

| Important role in the story | |
|---|---|
| Past experiences that shaped who they are | |
| Character Arc | Notes |

- ☐ Accountable
- ☐ Adaptable
- ☐ Adventurous
- ☐ Affable
- ☐ Alert
- ☐ Ambitious
- ☐ Appropriate
- ☐ Arrogant
- ☐ Assertive
- ☐ Astute
- ☐ Attentive
- ☐ Authentic
- ☐ Boorish
- ☐ Bossy
- ☐ Bravery
- ☐ Calm
- ☐ Candid
- ☐ Capable
- ☐ Charismatic
- ☐ Charming
- ☐ Collaborative
- ☐ Committed
- ☐ Communicator
- ☐ Compassionate
- ☐ Conceited
- ☐ Confident
- ☐ Connected
- ☐ Conscientious
- ☐ Considerate
- ☐ Consistent
- ☐ Cooperative
- ☐ Courageous
- ☐ Cowardly
- ☐ Creative
- ☐ Cultured
- ☐ Curious
- ☐ Dedicated
- ☐ Dependable
- ☐ Determined

- ☐ Diplomatic
- ☐ Disciplined
- ☐ Discreet
- ☐ Dishonest
- ☐ Dutiful
- ☐ Easygoing
- ☐ Efficient
- ☐ Empathetic
- ☐ Encouraging
- ☐ Energetic
- ☐ Enthusiastic
- ☐ Ethical
- ☐ Expressive
- ☐ Exuberant
- ☐ Facilitates
- ☐ Fair
- ☐ Fairness
- ☐ Faithful
- ☐ Fearless
- ☐ Finicky
- ☐ Flexible
- ☐ Friendly
- ☐ Generative
- ☐ Generosity
- ☐ Gratitude
- ☐ Gregarious
- ☐ Happy
- ☐ Hard-Working
- ☐ Helpful
- ☐ Honest
- ☐ Honorable
- ☐ Humble
- ☐ Humorous
- ☐ Imaginative
- ☐ Immaculate
- ☐ Impartial
- ☐ Impulsive
- ☐ Independent
- ☐ Inquiring

- ☐ Innovative
- ☐ Intelligent
- ☐ Intentional
- ☐ Interested
- ☐ Intimate
- ☐ Joyful
- ☐ Keen
- ☐ Knowledgeable
- ☐ Lazy
- ☐ Listener
- ☐ Lively
- ☐ Logical
- ☐ Loving
- ☐ Loyal
- ☐ Malicious
- ☐ Meticulous
- ☐ Networker
- ☐ Nurturing
- ☐ Obnoxious
- ☐ Observant
- ☐ Open-Minded
- ☐ Optimistic
- ☐ Organized
- ☐ Patient
- ☐ Peaceful
- ☐ Persistent
- ☐ Picky
- ☐ Planner
- ☐ Playful
- ☐ Poised
- ☐ Polite
- ☐ Pompous
- ☐ Powerful
- ☐ Pragmatic
- ☐ Precise
- ☐ Proactive
- ☐ Problem-Solver
- ☐ Productive
- ☐ Punctual

- ☐ Quarrelsome
- ☐ Reliable
- ☐ Resourceful
- ☐ Responsible
- ☐ Rude
- ☐ Sarcastic
- ☐ Self-centered
- ☐ Self-confident
- ☐ Self-reliant
- ☐ Sense of Humor
- ☐ Sensual
- ☐ Serves Others
- ☐ Sincere
- ☐ Skillful
- ☐ Slovenly
- ☐ Sneaky
- ☐ Spiritual
- ☐ Spontaneous
- ☐ Stable
- ☐ Stingy
- ☐ Strong
- ☐ Successful
- ☐ Sullen
- ☐ Supportive
- ☐ Surly
- ☐ Tactful
- ☐ Thoughtless
- ☐ Trusting
- ☐ Trusting
- ☐ Trustworthy
- ☐ Truthful
- ☐ Unfriendly
- ☐ Unruly
- ☐ Versatile
- ☐ Vibrant
- ☐ Vulgar
- ☐ Warm
- ☐ Wise
- ☐ Zealous

| Name/Nicknames | | Age/Birthday | Race |
|---|---|---|---|
| Height/Weight | Gender/Sexuality | Eyes | Hair color |
| Parents | | Place of Birth | Species |
| Siblings | | Class/Status | Education |
| Where they have lived | | Schools Attended | |
| Clothes/Glasses/Scars | | Spiritual Beliefs | |
| Occupation | | Awards/Accomplishments | |
| Strongest personality characteristics | | Favorite activities/Hobbies | |
| People they love | | People they hate | |
| People they admire | | Pets | Hobbies |
| Problems | | Dreams and Ambitions | |

| | |
|---|---|
| *Important role in the story* | |
| *Past experiences that shaped who they are* | |

| | |
|---|---|
| Character Arc | Notes |

- Accountable
- Adaptable
- Adventurous
- Affable
- Alert
- Ambitious
- Appropriate
- Arrogant
- Assertive
- Astute
- Attentive
- Authentic
- Boorish
- Bossy
- Bravery
- Calm
- Candid
- Capable
- Charismatic
- Charming
- Collaborative
- Committed
- Communicator
- Compassionate
- Conceited
- Confident
- Connected
- Conscientious
- Considerate
- Consistent
- Cooperative
- Courageous
- Cowardly
- Creative
- Cultured
- Curious
- Dedicated
- Dependable
- Determined

- Diplomatic
- Disciplined
- Discreet
- Dishonest
- Dutiful
- Easygoing
- Efficient
- Empathetic
- Encouraging
- Energetic
- Enthusiastic
- Ethical
- Expressive
- Exuberant
- Facilitates
- Fair
- Fairness
- Faithful
- Fearless
- Finicky
- Flexible
- Friendly
- Generative
- Generosity
- Gratitude
- Gregarious
- Happy
- Hard-Working
- Helpful
- Honest
- Honorable
- Humble
- Humorous
- Imaginative
- Immaculate
- Impartial
- Impulsive
- Independent
- Inquiring

- Innovative
- Intelligent
- Intentional
- Interested
- Intimate
- Joyful
- Keen
- Knowledgeable
- Lazy
- Listener
- Lively
- Logical
- Loving
- Loyal
- Malicious
- Meticulous
- Networker
- Nurturing
- Obnoxious
- Observant
- Open-Minded
- Optimistic
- Organized
- Patient
- Peaceful
- Persistent
- Picky
- Planner
- Playful
- Poised
- Polite
- Pompous
- Powerful
- Pragmatic
- Precise
- Proactive
- Problem-Solver
- Productive
- Punctual

- Quarrelsome
- Reliable
- Resourceful
- Responsible
- Rude
- Sarcastic
- Self-centered
- Self-confident
- Self-reliant
- Sense of Humor
- Sensual
- Serves Others
- Sincere
- Skillful
- Slovenly
- Sneaky
- Spiritual
- Spontaneous
- Stable
- Stingy
- Strong
- Successful
- Sullen
- Supportive
- Surly
- Tactful
- Thoughtless
- Trusting
- Trusting
- Trustworthy
- Truthful
- Unfriendly
- Unruly
- Versatile
- Vibrant
- Vulgar
- Warm
- Wise
- Zealous

| Name/Nicknames | | Age/Birthday | Race |
| --- | --- | --- | --- |
| Height/Weight | Gender/Sexuality | Eyes | Hair color |
| Parents | | Place of Birth | Species |
| Siblings | | Class/Status | Education |
| Where they have lived | | Schools Attended | |
| Clothes/Glasses/Scars | | Spiritual Beliefs | |
| Occupation | | Awards/Accomplishments | |
| Strongest personality characteristics | | Favorite activities/Hobbies | |
| People they love | | People they hate | |
| People they admire | | Pets | Hobbies |
| Problems | | Dreams and Ambitions | |

*Important role in the story*

*Past experiences that shaped who they are*

| Character Arc | Notes |
|---|---|

- Accountable
- Adaptable
- Adventurous
- Affable
- Alert
- Ambitious
- Appropriate
- Arrogant
- Assertive
- Astute
- Attentive
- Authentic
- Boorish
- Bossy
- Bravery
- Calm
- Candid
- Capable
- Charismatic
- Charming
- Collaborative
- Committed
- Communicator
- Compassionate
- Conceited
- Confident
- Connected
- Conscientious
- Considerate
- Consistent
- Cooperative
- Courageous
- Cowardly
- Creative
- Cultured
- Curious
- Dedicated
- Dependable
- Determined
- Diplomatic
- Disciplined
- Discreet
- Dishonest
- Dutiful
- Easygoing
- Efficient
- Empathetic
- Encouraging
- Energetic
- Enthusiastic
- Ethical
- Expressive
- Exuberant
- Facilitates
- Fair
- Fairness
- Faithful
- Fearless
- Finicky
- Flexible
- Friendly
- Generative
- Generosity
- Gratitude
- Gregarious
- Happy
- Hard-Working
- Helpful
- Honest
- Honorable
- Humble
- Humorous
- Imaginative
- Immaculate
- Impartial
- Impulsive
- Independent
- Inquiring
- Innovative
- Intelligent
- Intentional
- Interested
- Intimate
- Joyful
- Keen
- Knowledgeable
- Lazy
- Listener
- Lively
- Logical
- Loving
- Loyal
- Malicious
- Meticulous
- Networker
- Nurturing
- Obnoxious
- Observant
- Open-Minded
- Optimistic
- Organized
- Patient
- Peaceful
- Persistent
- Picky
- Planner
- Playful
- Poised
- Polite
- Pompous
- Powerful
- Pragmatic
- Precise
- Proactive
- Problem-Solver
- Productive
- Punctual
- Quarrelsome
- Reliable
- Resourceful
- Responsible
- Rude
- Sarcastic
- Self-centered
- Self-confident
- Self-reliant
- Sense of Humor
- Sensual
- Serves Others
- Sincere
- Skillful
- Slovenly
- Sneaky
- Spiritual
- Spontaneous
- Stable
- Stingy
- Strong
- Successful
- Sullen
- Supportive
- Surly
- Tactful
- Thoughtless
- Trusting
- Trusting
- Trustworthy
- Truthful
- Unfriendly
- Unruly
- Versatile
- Vibrant
- Vulgar
- Warm
- Wise
- Zealous

| Name/Nicknames | | Age/Birthday | Race |
| --- | --- | --- | --- |
| Height/Weight | Gender/Sexuality | Eyes | Hair color |
| Parents | | Place of Birth | Species |
| Siblings | | Class/Status | Education |
| Where they have lived | | Schools Attended | |
| Clothes/Glasses/Scars | | Spiritual Beliefs | |
| Occupation | | Awards/Accomplishments | |
| Strongest personality characteristics | | Favorite activities/Hobbies | |
| People they love | | People they hate | |
| People they admire | | Pets | Hobbies |
| Problems | | Dreams and Ambitions | |

| Important role in the story | |
|---|---|
| Past experiences that shaped who they are | |

| Character Arc | Notes |
|---|---|
| | |

| | | | | | | | |
|---|---|---|---|---|---|---|---|
| o | Accountable | o | Diplomatic | o | Innovative | o | Quarrelsome |
| o | Adaptable | o | Disciplined | o | Intelligent | o | Reliable |
| o | Adventurous | o | Discreet | o | Intentional | o | Resourceful |
| o | Affable | o | Dishonest | o | Interested | o | Responsible |
| o | Alert | o | Dutiful | o | Intimate | o | Rude |
| o | Ambitious | o | Easygoing | o | Joyful | o | Sarcastic |
| o | Appropriate | o | Efficient | o | Keen | o | Self-centered |
| o | Arrogant | o | Empathetic | o | Knowledgeable | o | Self-confident |
| o | Assertive | o | Encouraging | o | Lazy | o | Self-reliant |
| o | Astute | o | Energetic | o | Listener | o | Sense of Humor |
| o | Attentive | o | Enthusiastic | o | Lively | o | Sensual |
| o | Authentic | o | Ethical | o | Logical | o | Serves Others |
| o | Boorish | o | Expressive | o | Loving | o | Sincere |
| o | Bossy | o | Exuberant | o | Loyal | o | Skillful |
| o | Bravery | o | Facilitates | o | Malicious | o | Slovenly |
| o | Calm | o | Fair | o | Meticulous | o | Sneaky |
| o | Candid | o | Fairness | o | Networker | o | Spiritual |
| o | Capable | o | Faithful | o | Nurturing | o | Spontaneous |
| o | Charismatic | o | Fearless | o | Obnoxious | o | Stable |
| o | Charming | o | Finicky | o | Observant | o | Stingy |
| o | Collaborative | o | Flexible | o | Open-Minded | o | Strong |
| o | Committed | o | Friendly | o | Optimistic | o | Successful |
| o | Communicator | o | Generative | o | Organized | o | Sullen |
| o | Compassionate | o | Generosity | o | Patient | o | Supportive |
| o | Conceited | o | Gratitude | o | Peaceful | o | Surly |
| o | Confident | o | Gregarious | o | Persistent | o | Tactful |
| o | Connected | o | Happy | o | Picky | o | Thoughtless |
| o | Conscientious | o | Hard-Working | o | Planner | o | Trusting |
| o | Considerate | o | Helpful | o | Playful | o | Trusting |
| o | Consistent | o | Honest | o | Poised | o | Trustworthy |
| o | Cooperative | o | Honorable | o | Polite | o | Truthful |
| o | Courageous | o | Humble | o | Pompous | o | Unfriendly |
| o | Cowardly | o | Humorous | o | Powerful | o | Unruly |
| o | Creative | o | Imaginative | o | Pragmatic | o | Versatile |
| o | Cultured | o | Immaculate | o | Precise | o | Vibrant |
| o | Curious | o | Impartial | o | Proactive | o | Vulgar |
| o | Dedicated | o | Impulsive | o | Problem-Solver | o | Warm |
| o | Dependable | o | Independent | o | Productive | o | Wise |
| o | Determined | o | Inquiring | o | Punctual | o | Zealous |

| Name/Nicknames | | Age/Birthday | Race |
|---|---|---|---|
| Height/Weight | Gender/Sexuality | Eyes | Hair color |
| Parents | | Place of Birth | Species |
| Siblings | | Class/Status | Education |
| Where they have lived | | Schools Attended | |
| Clothes/Glasses/Scars | | Spiritual Beliefs | |
| Occupation | | Awards/Accomplishments | |
| Strongest personality characteristics | | Favorite activities/Hobbies | |
| People they love | | People they hate | |
| People they admire | | Pets | Hobbies |
| Problems | | Dreams and Ambitions | |

| Important role in the story | |
|---|---|
| Past experiences that shaped who they are | |
| Character Arc | Notes |

- Accountable
- Adaptable
- Adventurous
- Affable
- Alert
- Ambitious
- Appropriate
- Arrogant
- Assertive
- Astute
- Attentive
- Authentic
- Boorish
- Bossy
- Bravery
- Calm
- Candid
- Capable
- Charismatic
- Charming
- Collaborative
- Committed
- Communicator
- Compassionate
- Conceited
- Confident
- Connected
- Conscientious
- Considerate
- Consistent
- Cooperative
- Courageous
- Cowardly
- Creative
- Cultured
- Curious
- Dedicated
- Dependable
- Determined
- Diplomatic
- Disciplined
- Discreet
- Dishonest
- Dutiful
- Easygoing
- Efficient
- Empathetic
- Encouraging
- Energetic
- Enthusiastic
- Ethical
- Expressive
- Exuberant
- Facilitates
- Fair
- Fairness
- Faithful
- Fearless
- Finicky
- Flexible
- Friendly
- Generative
- Generosity
- Gratitude
- Gregarious
- Happy
- Hard-Working
- Helpful
- Honest
- Honorable
- Humble
- Humorous
- Imaginative
- Immaculate
- Impartial
- Impulsive
- Independent
- Inquiring
- Innovative
- Intelligent
- Intentional
- Interested
- Intimate
- Joyful
- Keen
- Knowledgeable
- Lazy
- Listener
- Lively
- Logical
- Loving
- Loyal
- Malicious
- Meticulous
- Networker
- Nurturing
- Obnoxious
- Observant
- Open-Minded
- Optimistic
- Organized
- Patient
- Peaceful
- Persistent
- Picky
- Planner
- Playful
- Poised
- Polite
- Pompous
- Powerful
- Pragmatic
- Precise
- Proactive
- Problem-Solver
- Productive
- Punctual
- Quarrelsome
- Reliable
- Resourceful
- Responsible
- Rude
- Sarcastic
- Self-centered
- Self-confident
- Self-reliant
- Sense of Humor
- Sensual
- Serves Others
- Sincere
- Skillful
- Slovenly
- Sneaky
- Spiritual
- Spontaneous
- Stable
- Stingy
- Strong
- Successful
- Sullen
- Supportive
- Surly
- Tactful
- Thoughtless
- Trusting
- Trusting
- Trustworthy
- Truthful
- Unfriendly
- Unruly
- Versatile
- Vibrant
- Vulgar
- Warm
- Wise
- Zealous

| Name/Nicknames | | Age/Birthday | Race |
| --- | --- | --- | --- |
| Height/Weight | Gender/Sexuality | Eyes | Hair color |
| Parents | | Place of Birth | Species |
| Siblings | | Class/Status | Education |
| Where they have lived | | Schools Attended | |
| Clothes/Glasses/Scars | | Spiritual Beliefs | |
| Occupation | | Awards/Accomplishments | |
| Strongest personality characteristics | | Favorite activities/Hobbies | |
| People they love | | People they hate | |
| People they admire | | Pets | Hobbies |
| Problems | | Dreams and Ambitions | |

| *Important role in the story* | |
|---|---|
| *Past experiences that shaped who they are* | |

| Character Arc | Notes |
|---|---|
| | |

| | | | | | | | |
|---|---|---|---|---|---|---|---|
| o | Accountable | o | Diplomatic | o | Innovative | o | Quarrelsome |
| o | Adaptable | o | Disciplined | o | Intelligent | o | Reliable |
| o | Adventurous | o | Discreet | o | Intentional | o | Resourceful |
| o | Affable | o | Dishonest | o | Interested | o | Responsible |
| o | Alert | o | Dutiful | o | Intimate | o | Rude |
| o | Ambitious | o | Easygoing | o | Joyful | o | Sarcastic |
| o | Appropriate | o | Efficient | o | Keen | o | Self-centered |
| o | Arrogant | o | Empathetic | o | Knowledgeable | o | Self-confident |
| o | Assertive | o | Encouraging | o | Lazy | o | Self-reliant |
| o | Astute | o | Energetic | o | Listener | o | Sense of Humor |
| o | Attentive | o | Enthusiastic | o | Lively | o | Sensual |
| o | Authentic | o | Ethical | o | Logical | o | Serves Others |
| o | Boorish | o | Expressive | o | Loving | o | Sincere |
| o | Bossy | o | Exuberant | o | Loyal | o | Skillful |
| o | Bravery | o | Facilitates | o | Malicious | o | Slovenly |
| o | Calm | o | Fair | o | Meticulous | o | Sneaky |
| o | Candid | o | Fairness | o | Networker | o | Spiritual |
| o | Capable | o | Faithful | o | Nurturing | o | Spontaneous |
| o | Charismatic | o | Fearless | o | Obnoxious | o | Stable |
| o | Charming | o | Finicky | o | Observant | o | Stingy |
| o | Collaborative | o | Flexible | o | Open-Minded | o | Strong |
| o | Committed | o | Friendly | o | Optimistic | o | Successful |
| o | Communicator | o | Generative | o | Organized | o | Sullen |
| o | Compassionate | o | Generosity | o | Patient | o | Supportive |
| o | Conceited | o | Gratitude | o | Peaceful | o | Surly |
| o | Confident | o | Gregarious | o | Persistent | o | Tactful |
| o | Connected | o | Happy | o | Picky | o | Thoughtless |
| o | Conscientious | o | Hard-Working | o | Planner | o | Trusting |
| o | Considerate | o | Helpful | o | Playful | o | Trusting |
| o | Consistent | o | Honest | o | Poised | o | Trustworthy |
| o | Cooperative | o | Honorable | o | Polite | o | Truthful |
| o | Courageous | o | Humble | o | Pompous | o | Unfriendly |
| o | Cowardly | o | Humorous | o | Powerful | o | Unruly |
| o | Creative | o | Imaginative | o | Pragmatic | o | Versatile |
| o | Cultured | o | Immaculate | o | Precise | o | Vibrant |
| o | Curious | o | Impartial | o | Proactive | o | Vulgar |
| o | Dedicated | o | Impulsive | o | Problem-Solver | o | Warm |
| o | Dependable | o | Independent | o | Productive | o | Wise |
| o | Determined | o | Inquiring | o | Punctual | o | Zealous |

| Name/Nicknames | | Age/Birthday | Race |
| --- | --- | --- | --- |
| Height/Weight | Gender/Sexuality | Eyes | Hair color |
| Parents | | Place of Birth | Species |
| Siblings | | Class/Status | Education |
| Where they have lived | | Schools Attended | |
| Clothes/Glasses/Scars | | Spiritual Beliefs | |
| Occupation | | Awards/Accomplishments | |
| Strongest personality characteristics | | Favorite activities/Hobbies | |
| People they love | | People they hate | |
| People they admire | | Pets | Hobbies |
| Problems | | Dreams and Ambitions | |

| Important role in the story | |
|---|---|
| Past experiences that shaped who they are | |
| Character Arc | Notes |

- Accountable
- Adaptable
- Adventurous
- Affable
- Alert
- Ambitious
- Appropriate
- Arrogant
- Assertive
- Astute
- Attentive
- Authentic
- Boorish
- Bossy
- Bravery
- Calm
- Candid
- Capable
- Charismatic
- Charming
- Collaborative
- Committed
- Communicator
- Compassionate
- Conceited
- Confident
- Connected
- Conscientious
- Considerate
- Consistent
- Cooperative
- Courageous
- Cowardly
- Creative
- Cultured
- Curious
- Dedicated
- Dependable
- Determined
- Diplomatic
- Disciplined
- Discreet
- Dishonest
- Dutiful
- Easygoing
- Efficient
- Empathetic
- Encouraging
- Energetic
- Enthusiastic
- Ethical
- Expressive
- Exuberant
- Facilitates
- Fair
- Fairness
- Faithful
- Fearless
- Finicky
- Flexible
- Friendly
- Generative
- Generosity
- Gratitude
- Gregarious
- Happy
- Hard-Working
- Helpful
- Honest
- Honorable
- Humble
- Humorous
- Imaginative
- Immaculate
- Impartial
- Impulsive
- Independent
- Inquiring
- Innovative
- Intelligent
- Intentional
- Interested
- Intimate
- Joyful
- Keen
- Knowledgeable
- Lazy
- Listener
- Lively
- Logical
- Loving
- Loyal
- Malicious
- Meticulous
- Networker
- Nurturing
- Obnoxious
- Observant
- Open-Minded
- Optimistic
- Organized
- Patient
- Peaceful
- Persistent
- Picky
- Planner
- Playful
- Poised
- Polite
- Pompous
- Powerful
- Pragmatic
- Precise
- Proactive
- Problem-Solver
- Productive
- Punctual
- Quarrelsome
- Reliable
- Resourceful
- Responsible
- Rude
- Sarcastic
- Self-centered
- Self-confident
- Self-reliant
- Sense of Humor
- Sensual
- Serves Others
- Sincere
- Skillful
- Slovenly
- Sneaky
- Spiritual
- Spontaneous
- Stable
- Stingy
- Strong
- Successful
- Sullen
- Supportive
- Surly
- Tactful
- Thoughtless
- Trusting
- Trusting
- Trustworthy
- Truthful
- Unfriendly
- Unruly
- Versatile
- Vibrant
- Vulgar
- Warm
- Wise
- Zealous

| Name/Nicknames | | Age/Birthday | Race |
|---|---|---|---|
| Height/Weight | Gender/Sexuality | Eyes | Hair color |
| Parents | | Place of Birth | Species |
| Siblings | | Class/Status | Education |
| Where they have lived | | Schools Attended | |
| Clothes/Glasses/Scars | | Spiritual Beliefs | |
| Occupation | | Awards/Accomplishments | |
| Strongest personality characteristics | | Favorite activities/Hobbies | |
| People they love | | People they hate | |
| People they admire | | Pets | Hobbies |
| Problems | | Dreams and Ambitions | |

| Important role in the story | |
|---|---|
| Past experiences that shaped who they are | |

| Character Arc | Notes |
|---|---|
| | |

| | | | |
|---|---|---|---|
| o Accountable | o Diplomatic | o Innovative | o Quarrelsome |
| o Adaptable | o Disciplined | o Intelligent | o Reliable |
| o Adventurous | o Discreet | o Intentional | o Resourceful |
| o Affable | o Dishonest | o Interested | o Responsible |
| o Alert | o Dutiful | o Intimate | o Rude |
| o Ambitious | o Easygoing | o Joyful | o Sarcastic |
| o Appropriate | o Efficient | o Keen | o Self-centered |
| o Arrogant | o Empathetic | o Knowledgeable | o Self-confident |
| o Assertive | o Encouraging | o Lazy | o Self-reliant |
| o Astute | o Energetic | o Listener | o Sense of Humor |
| o Attentive | o Enthusiastic | o Lively | o Sensual |
| o Authentic | o Ethical | o Logical | o Serves Others |
| o Boorish | o Expressive | o Loving | o Sincere |
| o Bossy | o Exuberant | o Loyal | o Skillful |
| o Bravery | o Facilitates | o Malicious | o Slovenly |
| o Calm | o Fair | o Meticulous | o Sneaky |
| o Candid | o Fairness | o Networker | o Spiritual |
| o Capable | o Faithful | o Nurturing | o Spontaneous |
| o Charismatic | o Fearless | o Obnoxious | o Stable |
| o Charming | o Finicky | o Observant | o Stingy |
| o Collaborative | o Flexible | o Open-Minded | o Strong |
| o Committed | o Friendly | o Optimistic | o Successful |
| o Communicator | o Generative | o Organized | o Sullen |
| o Compassionate | o Generosity | o Patient | o Supportive |
| o Conceited | o Gratitude | o Peaceful | o Surly |
| o Confident | o Gregarious | o Persistent | o Tactful |
| o Connected | o Happy | o Picky | o Thoughtless |
| o Conscientious | o Hard-Working | o Planner | o Trusting |
| o Considerate | o Helpful | o Playful | o Trusting |
| o Consistent | o Honest | o Poised | o Trustworthy |
| o Cooperative | o Honorable | o Polite | o Truthful |
| o Courageous | o Humble | o Pompous | o Unfriendly |
| o Cowardly | o Humorous | o Powerful | o Unruly |
| o Creative | o Imaginative | o Pragmatic | o Versatile |
| o Cultured | o Immaculate | o Precise | o Vibrant |
| o Curious | o Impartial | o Proactive | o Vulgar |
| o Dedicated | o Impulsive | o Problem-Solver | o Warm |
| o Dependable | o Independent | o Productive | o Wise |
| o Determined | o Inquiring | o Punctual | o Zealous |

| Name/Nicknames | | Age/Birthday | Race |
|---|---|---|---|
| Height/Weight | Gender/Sexuality | Eyes | Hair color |
| Parents | | Place of Birth | Species |
| Siblings | | Class/Status | Education |
| Where they have lived | | Schools Attended | |
| Clothes/Glasses/Scars | | Spiritual Beliefs | |
| Occupation | | Awards/Accomplishments | |
| Strongest personality characteristics | | Favorite activities/Hobbies | |
| People they love | | People they hate | |
| People they admire | | Pets | Hobbies |
| Problems | | Dreams and Ambitions | |

| Important role in the story | |
|---|---|
| Past experiences that shaped who they are | |
| Character Arc | Notes |

- Accountable
- Adaptable
- Adventurous
- Affable
- Alert
- Ambitious
- Appropriate
- Arrogant
- Assertive
- Astute
- Attentive
- Authentic
- Boorish
- Bossy
- Bravery
- Calm
- Candid
- Capable
- Charismatic
- Charming
- Collaborative
- Committed
- Communicator
- Compassionate
- Conceited
- Confident
- Connected
- Conscientious
- Considerate
- Consistent
- Cooperative
- Courageous
- Cowardly
- Creative
- Cultured
- Curious
- Dedicated
- Dependable
- Determined
- Diplomatic
- Disciplined
- Discreet
- Dishonest
- Dutiful
- Easygoing
- Efficient
- Empathetic
- Encouraging
- Energetic
- Enthusiastic
- Ethical
- Expressive
- Exuberant
- Facilitates
- Fair
- Fairness
- Faithful
- Fearless
- Finicky
- Flexible
- Friendly
- Generative
- Generosity
- Gratitude
- Gregarious
- Happy
- Hard-Working
- Helpful
- Honest
- Honorable
- Humble
- Humorous
- Imaginative
- Immaculate
- Impartial
- Impulsive
- Independent
- Inquiring
- Innovative
- Intelligent
- Intentional
- Interested
- Intimate
- Joyful
- Keen
- Knowledgeable
- Lazy
- Listener
- Lively
- Logical
- Loving
- Loyal
- Malicious
- Meticulous
- Networker
- Nurturing
- Obnoxious
- Observant
- Open-Minded
- Optimistic
- Organized
- Patient
- Peaceful
- Persistent
- Picky
- Planner
- Playful
- Poised
- Polite
- Pompous
- Powerful
- Pragmatic
- Precise
- Proactive
- Problem-Solver
- Productive
- Punctual
- Quarrelsome
- Reliable
- Resourceful
- Responsible
- Rude
- Sarcastic
- Self-centered
- Self-confident
- Self-reliant
- Sense of Humor
- Sensual
- Serves Others
- Sincere
- Skillful
- Slovenly
- Sneaky
- Spiritual
- Spontaneous
- Stable
- Stingy
- Strong
- Successful
- Sullen
- Supportive
- Surly
- Tactful
- Thoughtless
- Trusting
- Trusting
- Trustworthy
- Truthful
- Unfriendly
- Unruly
- Versatile
- Vibrant
- Vulgar
- Warm
- Wise
- Zealous

| Name/Nicknames | | Age/Birthday | Race |
|---|---|---|---|
| Height/Weight | Gender/Sexuality | Eyes | Hair color |
| Parents | | Place of Birth | Species |
| Siblings | | Class/Status | Education |
| Where they have lived | | Schools Attended | |
| Clothes/Glasses/Scars | | Spiritual Beliefs | |
| Occupation | | Awards/Accomplishments | |
| Strongest personality characteristics | | Favorite activities/Hobbies | |
| People they love | | People they hate | |
| People they admire | | Pets | Hobbies |
| Problems | | Dreams and Ambitions | |

| Important role in the story | |
|---|---|
| Past experiences that shaped who they are | |
| Character Arc | Notes |

- Accountable
- Adaptable
- Adventurous
- Affable
- Alert
- Ambitious
- Appropriate
- Arrogant
- Assertive
- Astute
- Attentive
- Authentic
- Boorish
- Bossy
- Bravery
- Calm
- Candid
- Capable
- Charismatic
- Charming
- Collaborative
- Committed
- Communicator
- Compassionate
- Conceited
- Confident
- Connected
- Conscientious
- Considerate
- Consistent
- Cooperative
- Courageous
- Cowardly
- Creative
- Cultured
- Curious
- Dedicated
- Dependable
- Determined
- Diplomatic
- Disciplined
- Discreet
- Dishonest
- Dutiful
- Easygoing
- Efficient
- Empathetic
- Encouraging
- Energetic
- Enthusiastic
- Ethical
- Expressive
- Exuberant
- Facilitates
- Fair
- Fairness
- Faithful
- Fearless
- Finicky
- Flexible
- Friendly
- Generative
- Generosity
- Gratitude
- Gregarious
- Happy
- Hard-Working
- Helpful
- Honest
- Honorable
- Humble
- Humorous
- Imaginative
- Immaculate
- Impartial
- Impulsive
- Independent
- Inquiring
- Innovative
- Intelligent
- Intentional
- Interested
- Intimate
- Joyful
- Keen
- Knowledgeable
- Lazy
- Listener
- Lively
- Logical
- Loving
- Loyal
- Malicious
- Meticulous
- Networker
- Nurturing
- Obnoxious
- Observant
- Open-Minded
- Optimistic
- Organized
- Patient
- Peaceful
- Persistent
- Picky
- Planner
- Playful
- Poised
- Polite
- Pompous
- Powerful
- Pragmatic
- Precise
- Proactive
- Problem-Solver
- Productive
- Punctual
- Quarrelsome
- Reliable
- Resourceful
- Responsible
- Rude
- Sarcastic
- Self-centered
- Self-confident
- Self-reliant
- Sense of Humor
- Sensual
- Serves Others
- Sincere
- Skillful
- Slovenly
- Sneaky
- Spiritual
- Spontaneous
- Stable
- Stingy
- Strong
- Successful
- Sullen
- Supportive
- Surly
- Tactful
- Thoughtless
- Trusting
- Trusting
- Trustworthy
- Truthful
- Unfriendly
- Unruly
- Versatile
- Vibrant
- Vulgar
- Warm
- Wise
- Zealous

| Name/Nicknames | | Age/Birthday | Race |
| --- | --- | --- | --- |
| Height/Weight | Gender/Sexuality | Eyes | Hair color |
| Parents | | Place of Birth | Species |
| Siblings | | Class/Status | Education |
| Where they have lived | | Schools Attended | |
| Clothes/Glasses/Scars | | Spiritual Beliefs | |
| Occupation | | Awards/Accomplishments | |
| Strongest personality characteristics | | Favorite activities/Hobbies | |
| People they love | | People they hate | |
| People they admire | | Pets | Hobbies |
| Problems | | Dreams and Ambitions | |

| Important role in the story | |
|---|---|
| Past experiences that shaped who they are | |
| Character Arc | Notes |

- Accountable
- Adaptable
- Adventurous
- Affable
- Alert
- Ambitious
- Appropriate
- Arrogant
- Assertive
- Astute
- Attentive
- Authentic
- Boorish
- Bossy
- Bravery
- Calm
- Candid
- Capable
- Charismatic
- Charming
- Collaborative
- Committed
- Communicator
- Compassionate
- Conceited
- Confident
- Connected
- Conscientious
- Considerate
- Consistent
- Cooperative
- Courageous
- Cowardly
- Creative
- Cultured
- Curious
- Dedicated
- Dependable
- Determined
- Diplomatic
- Disciplined
- Discreet
- Dishonest
- Dutiful
- Easygoing
- Efficient
- Empathetic
- Encouraging
- Energetic
- Enthusiastic
- Ethical
- Expressive
- Exuberant
- Facilitates
- Fair
- Fairness
- Faithful
- Fearless
- Finicky
- Flexible
- Friendly
- Generative
- Generosity
- Gratitude
- Gregarious
- Happy
- Hard-Working
- Helpful
- Honest
- Honorable
- Humble
- Humorous
- Imaginative
- Immaculate
- Impartial
- Impulsive
- Independent
- Inquiring
- Innovative
- Intelligent
- Intentional
- Interested
- Intimate
- Joyful
- Keen
- Knowledgeable
- Lazy
- Listener
- Lively
- Logical
- Loving
- Loyal
- Malicious
- Meticulous
- Networker
- Nurturing
- Obnoxious
- Observant
- Open-Minded
- Optimistic
- Organized
- Patient
- Peaceful
- Persistent
- Picky
- Planner
- Playful
- Poised
- Polite
- Pompous
- Powerful
- Pragmatic
- Precise
- Proactive
- Problem-Solver
- Productive
- Punctual
- Quarrelsome
- Reliable
- Resourceful
- Responsible
- Rude
- Sarcastic
- Self-centered
- Self-confident
- Self-reliant
- Sense of Humor
- Sensual
- Serves Others
- Sincere
- Skillful
- Slovenly
- Sneaky
- Spiritual
- Spontaneous
- Stable
- Stingy
- Strong
- Successful
- Sullen
- Supportive
- Surly
- Tactful
- Thoughtless
- Trusting
- Trusting
- Trustworthy
- Truthful
- Unfriendly
- Unruly
- Versatile
- Vibrant
- Vulgar
- Warm
- Wise
- Zealous

| Name/Nicknames | | Age/Birthday | Race |
| --- | --- | --- | --- |
| Height/Weight | Gender/Sexuality | Eyes | Hair color |
| Parents | | Place of Birth | Species |
| Siblings | | Class/Status | Education |
| Where they have lived | | Schools Attended | |
| Clothes/Glasses/Scars | | Spiritual Beliefs | |
| Occupation | | Awards/Accomplishments | |
| Strongest personality characteristics | | Favorite activities/Hobbies | |
| People they love | | People they hate | |
| People they admire | | Pets | Hobbies |
| Problems | | Dreams and Ambitions | |

| Important role in the story | |
|---|---|
| Past experiences that shaped who they are | |

| Character Arc | Notes |
|---|---|
| | |

- ○ Accountable
- ○ Adaptable
- ○ Adventurous
- ○ Affable
- ○ Alert
- ○ Ambitious
- ○ Appropriate
- ○ Arrogant
- ○ Assertive
- ○ Astute
- ○ Attentive
- ○ Authentic
- ○ Boorish
- ○ Bossy
- ○ Bravery
- ○ Calm
- ○ Candid
- ○ Capable
- ○ Charismatic
- ○ Charming
- ○ Collaborative
- ○ Committed
- ○ Communicator
- ○ Compassionate
- ○ Conceited
- ○ Confident
- ○ Connected
- ○ Conscientious
- ○ Considerate
- ○ Consistent
- ○ Cooperative
- ○ Courageous
- ○ Cowardly
- ○ Creative
- ○ Cultured
- ○ Curious
- ○ Dedicated
- ○ Dependable
- ○ Determined

- ○ Diplomatic
- ○ Disciplined
- ○ Discreet
- ○ Dishonest
- ○ Dutiful
- ○ Easygoing
- ○ Efficient
- ○ Empathetic
- ○ Encouraging
- ○ Energetic
- ○ Enthusiastic
- ○ Ethical
- ○ Expressive
- ○ Exuberant
- ○ Facilitates
- ○ Fair
- ○ Fairness
- ○ Faithful
- ○ Fearless
- ○ Finicky
- ○ Flexible
- ○ Friendly
- ○ Generative
- ○ Generosity
- ○ Gratitude
- ○ Gregarious
- ○ Happy
- ○ Hard-Working
- ○ Helpful
- ○ Honest
- ○ Honorable
- ○ Humble
- ○ Humorous
- ○ Imaginative
- ○ Immaculate
- ○ Impartial
- ○ Impulsive
- ○ Independent
- ○ Inquiring

- ○ Innovative
- ○ Intelligent
- ○ Intentional
- ○ Interested
- ○ Intimate
- ○ Joyful
- ○ Keen
- ○ Knowledgeable
- ○ Lazy
- ○ Listener
- ○ Lively
- ○ Logical
- ○ Loving
- ○ Loyal
- ○ Malicious
- ○ Meticulous
- ○ Networker
- ○ Nurturing
- ○ Obnoxious
- ○ Observant
- ○ Open-Minded
- ○ Optimistic
- ○ Organized
- ○ Patient
- ○ Peaceful
- ○ Persistent
- ○ Picky
- ○ Planner
- ○ Playful
- ○ Poised
- ○ Polite
- ○ Pompous
- ○ Powerful
- ○ Pragmatic
- ○ Precise
- ○ Proactive
- ○ Problem-Solver
- ○ Productive
- ○ Punctual

- ○ Quarrelsome
- ○ Reliable
- ○ Resourceful
- ○ Responsible
- ○ Rude
- ○ Sarcastic
- ○ Self-centered
- ○ Self-confident
- ○ Self-reliant
- ○ Sense of Humor
- ○ Sensual
- ○ Serves Others
- ○ Sincere
- ○ Skillful
- ○ Slovenly
- ○ Sneaky
- ○ Spiritual
- ○ Spontaneous
- ○ Stable
- ○ Stingy
- ○ Strong
- ○ Successful
- ○ Sullen
- ○ Supportive
- ○ Surly
- ○ Tactful
- ○ Thoughtless
- ○ Trusting
- ○ Trusting
- ○ Trustworthy
- ○ Truthful
- ○ Unfriendly
- ○ Unruly
- ○ Versatile
- ○ Vibrant
- ○ Vulgar
- ○ Warm
- ○ Wise
- ○ Zealous

| Name/Nicknames | | Age/Birthday | Race |
| --- | --- | --- | --- |
| Height/Weight | Gender/Sexuality | Eyes | Hair color |
| Parents | | Place of Birth | Species |
| Siblings | | Class/Status | Education |
| Where they have lived | | Schools Attended | |
| Clothes/Glasses/Scars | | Spiritual Beliefs | |
| Occupation | | Awards/Accomplishments | |
| Strongest personality characteristics | | Favorite activities/Hobbies | |
| People they love | | People they hate | |
| People they admire | | Pets | Hobbies |
| Problems | | Dreams and Ambitions | |

| Important role in the story | |
|---|---|
| Past experiences that shaped who they are | |
| Character Arc | Notes |

- Accountable
- Adaptable
- Adventurous
- Affable
- Alert
- Ambitious
- Appropriate
- Arrogant
- Assertive
- Astute
- Attentive
- Authentic
- Boorish
- Bossy
- Bravery
- Calm
- Candid
- Capable
- Charismatic
- Charming
- Collaborative
- Committed
- Communicator
- Compassionate
- Conceited
- Confident
- Connected
- Conscientious
- Considerate
- Consistent
- Cooperative
- Courageous
- Cowardly
- Creative
- Cultured
- Curious
- Dedicated
- Dependable
- Determined
- Diplomatic
- Disciplined
- Discreet
- Dishonest
- Dutiful
- Easygoing
- Efficient
- Empathetic
- Encouraging
- Energetic
- Enthusiastic
- Ethical
- Expressive
- Exuberant
- Facilitates
- Fair
- Fairness
- Faithful
- Fearless
- Finicky
- Flexible
- Friendly
- Generative
- Generosity
- Gratitude
- Gregarious
- Happy
- Hard-Working
- Helpful
- Honest
- Honorable
- Humble
- Humorous
- Imaginative
- Immaculate
- Impartial
- Impulsive
- Independent
- Inquiring
- Innovative
- Intelligent
- Intentional
- Interested
- Intimate
- Joyful
- Keen
- Knowledgeable
- Lazy
- Listener
- Lively
- Logical
- Loving
- Loyal
- Malicious
- Meticulous
- Networker
- Nurturing
- Obnoxious
- Observant
- Open-Minded
- Optimistic
- Organized
- Patient
- Peaceful
- Persistent
- Picky
- Planner
- Playful
- Poised
- Polite
- Pompous
- Powerful
- Pragmatic
- Precise
- Proactive
- Problem-Solver
- Productive
- Punctual
- Quarrelsome
- Reliable
- Resourceful
- Responsible
- Rude
- Sarcastic
- Self-centered
- Self-confident
- Self-reliant
- Sense of Humor
- Sensual
- Serves Others
- Sincere
- Skillful
- Slovenly
- Sneaky
- Spiritual
- Spontaneous
- Stable
- Stingy
- Strong
- Successful
- Sullen
- Supportive
- Surly
- Tactful
- Thoughtless
- Trusting
- Trusting
- Trustworthy
- Truthful
- Unfriendly
- Unruly
- Versatile
- Vibrant
- Vulgar
- Warm
- Wise
- Zealous

| Name/Nicknames | | Age/Birthday | Race |
|---|---|---|---|
| Height/Weight | Gender/Sexuality | Eyes | Hair color |
| Parents | | Place of Birth | Species |
| Siblings | | Class/Status | Education |
| Where they have lived | | Schools Attended | |
| Clothes/Glasses/Scars | | Spiritual Beliefs | |
| Occupation | | Awards/Accomplishments | |
| Strongest personality characteristics | | Favorite activities/Hobbies | |
| People they love | | People they hate | |
| People they admire | | Pets | Hobbies |
| Problems | | Dreams and Ambitions | |

| | |
|---|---|
| *Important role in the story* | |
| *Past experiences that shaped who they are* | |

| Character Arc | Notes |
|---|---|
| | |

- ○ Accountable
- ○ Adaptable
- ○ Adventurous
- ○ Affable
- ○ Alert
- ○ Ambitious
- ○ Appropriate
- ○ Arrogant
- ○ Assertive
- ○ Astute
- ○ Attentive
- ○ Authentic
- ○ Boorish
- ○ Bossy
- ○ Bravery
- ○ Calm
- ○ Candid
- ○ Capable
- ○ Charismatic
- ○ Charming
- ○ Collaborative
- ○ Committed
- ○ Communicator
- ○ Compassionate
- ○ Conceited
- ○ Confident
- ○ Connected
- ○ Conscientious
- ○ Considerate
- ○ Consistent
- ○ Cooperative
- ○ Courageous
- ○ Cowardly
- ○ Creative
- ○ Cultured
- ○ Curious
- ○ Dedicated
- ○ Dependable
- ○ Determined

- ○ Diplomatic
- ○ Disciplined
- ○ Discreet
- ○ Dishonest
- ○ Dutiful
- ○ Easygoing
- ○ Efficient
- ○ Empathetic
- ○ Encouraging
- ○ Energetic
- ○ Enthusiastic
- ○ Ethical
- ○ Expressive
- ○ Exuberant
- ○ Facilitates
- ○ Fair
- ○ Fairness
- ○ Faithful
- ○ Fearless
- ○ Finicky
- ○ Flexible
- ○ Friendly
- ○ Generative
- ○ Generosity
- ○ Gratitude
- ○ Gregarious
- ○ Happy
- ○ Hard-Working
- ○ Helpful
- ○ Honest
- ○ Honorable
- ○ Humble
- ○ Humorous
- ○ Imaginative
- ○ Immaculate
- ○ Impartial
- ○ Impulsive
- ○ Independent
- ○ Inquiring

- ○ Innovative
- ○ Intelligent
- ○ Intentional
- ○ Interested
- ○ Intimate
- ○ Joyful
- ○ Keen
- ○ Knowledgeable
- ○ Lazy
- ○ Listener
- ○ Lively
- ○ Logical
- ○ Loving
- ○ Loyal
- ○ Malicious
- ○ Meticulous
- ○ Networker
- ○ Nurturing
- ○ Obnoxious
- ○ Observant
- ○ Open-Minded
- ○ Optimistic
- ○ Organized
- ○ Patient
- ○ Peaceful
- ○ Persistent
- ○ Picky
- ○ Planner
- ○ Playful
- ○ Poised
- ○ Polite
- ○ Pompous
- ○ Powerful
- ○ Pragmatic
- ○ Precise
- ○ Proactive
- ○ Problem-Solver
- ○ Productive
- ○ Punctual

- ○ Quarrelsome
- ○ Reliable
- ○ Resourceful
- ○ Responsible
- ○ Rude
- ○ Sarcastic
- ○ Self-centered
- ○ Self-confident
- ○ Self-reliant
- ○ Sense of Humor
- ○ Sensual
- ○ Serves Others
- ○ Sincere
- ○ Skillful
- ○ Slovenly
- ○ Sneaky
- ○ Spiritual
- ○ Spontaneous
- ○ Stable
- ○ Stingy
- ○ Strong
- ○ Successful
- ○ Sullen
- ○ Supportive
- ○ Surly
- ○ Tactful
- ○ Thoughtless
- ○ Trusting
- ○ Trusting
- ○ Trustworthy
- ○ Truthful
- ○ Unfriendly
- ○ Unruly
- ○ Versatile
- ○ Vibrant
- ○ Vulgar
- ○ Warm
- ○ Wise
- ○ Zealous

| Name/Nicknames | | Age/Birthday | Race |
|---|---|---|---|
| Height/Weight | Gender/Sexuality | Eyes | Hair color |
| Parents | | Place of Birth | Species |
| Siblings | | Class/Status | Education |
| Where they have lived | | Schools Attended | |
| Clothes/Glasses/Scars | | Spiritual Beliefs | |
| Occupation | | Awards/Accomplishments | |
| Strongest personality characteristics | | Favorite activities/Hobbies | |
| People they love | | People they hate | |
| People they admire | | Pets | Hobbies |
| Problems | | Dreams and Ambitions | |

| Important role in the story | |
|---|---|
| **Past experiences that shaped who they are** | |
| **Character Arc** | **Notes** |

- Accountable
- Adaptable
- Adventurous
- Affable
- Alert
- Ambitious
- Appropriate
- Arrogant
- Assertive
- Astute
- Attentive
- Authentic
- Boorish
- Bossy
- Bravery
- Calm
- Candid
- Capable
- Charismatic
- Charming
- Collaborative
- Committed
- Communicator
- Compassionate
- Conceited
- Confident
- Connected
- Conscientious
- Considerate
- Consistent
- Cooperative
- Courageous
- Cowardly
- Creative
- Cultured
- Curious
- Dedicated
- Dependable
- Determined

- Diplomatic
- Disciplined
- Discreet
- Dishonest
- Dutiful
- Easygoing
- Efficient
- Empathetic
- Encouraging
- Energetic
- Enthusiastic
- Ethical
- Expressive
- Exuberant
- Facilitates
- Fair
- Fairness
- Faithful
- Fearless
- Finicky
- Flexible
- Friendly
- Generative
- Generosity
- Gratitude
- Gregarious
- Happy
- Hard-Working
- Helpful
- Honest
- Honorable
- Humble
- Humorous
- Imaginative
- Immaculate
- Impartial
- Impulsive
- Independent
- Inquiring

- Innovative
- Intelligent
- Intentional
- Interested
- Intimate
- Joyful
- Keen
- Knowledgeable
- Lazy
- Listener
- Lively
- Logical
- Loving
- Loyal
- Malicious
- Meticulous
- Networker
- Nurturing
- Obnoxious
- Observant
- Open-Minded
- Optimistic
- Organized
- Patient
- Peaceful
- Persistent
- Picky
- Planner
- Playful
- Poised
- Polite
- Pompous
- Powerful
- Pragmatic
- Precise
- Proactive
- Problem-Solver
- Productive
- Punctual

- Quarrelsome
- Reliable
- Resourceful
- Responsible
- Rude
- Sarcastic
- Self-centered
- Self-confident
- Self-reliant
- Sense of Humor
- Sensual
- Serves Others
- Sincere
- Skillful
- Slovenly
- Sneaky
- Spiritual
- Spontaneous
- Stable
- Stingy
- Strong
- Successful
- Sullen
- Supportive
- Surly
- Tactful
- Thoughtless
- Trusting
- Trusting
- Trustworthy
- Truthful
- Unfriendly
- Unruly
- Versatile
- Vibrant
- Vulgar
- Warm
- Wise
- Zealous

| Name/Nicknames | | Age/Birthday | Race |
|---|---|---|---|
| Height/Weight | Gender/Sexuality | Eyes | Hair color |
| Parents | | Place of Birth | Species |
| Siblings | | Class/Status | Education |
| Where they have lived | | Schools Attended | |
| Clothes/Glasses/Scars | | Spiritual Beliefs | |
| Occupation | | Awards/Accomplishments | |
| Strongest personality characteristics | | Favorite activities/Hobbies | |
| People they love | | People they hate | |
| People they admire | | Pets | Hobbies |
| Problems | | Dreams and Ambitions | |

| | |
|---|---|
| *Important role in the story* | |
| *Past experiences that shaped who they are* | |

| Character Arc | Notes |
|---|---|
| | |

- Accountable
- Adaptable
- Adventurous
- Affable
- Alert
- Ambitious
- Appropriate
- Arrogant
- Assertive
- Astute
- Attentive
- Authentic
- Boorish
- Bossy
- Bravery
- Calm
- Candid
- Capable
- Charismatic
- Charming
- Collaborative
- Committed
- Communicator
- Compassionate
- Conceited
- Confident
- Connected
- Conscientious
- Considerate
- Consistent
- Cooperative
- Courageous
- Cowardly
- Creative
- Cultured
- Curious
- Dedicated
- Dependable
- Determined
- Diplomatic
- Disciplined
- Discreet
- Dishonest
- Dutiful
- Easygoing
- Efficient
- Empathetic
- Encouraging
- Energetic
- Enthusiastic
- Ethical
- Expressive
- Exuberant
- Facilitates
- Fair
- Fairness
- Faithful
- Fearless
- Finicky
- Flexible
- Friendly
- Generative
- Generosity
- Gratitude
- Gregarious
- Happy
- Hard-Working
- Helpful
- Honest
- Honorable
- Humble
- Humorous
- Imaginative
- Immaculate
- Impartial
- Impulsive
- Independent
- Inquiring
- Innovative
- Intelligent
- Intentional
- Interested
- Intimate
- Joyful
- Keen
- Knowledgeable
- Lazy
- Listener
- Lively
- Logical
- Loving
- Loyal
- Malicious
- Meticulous
- Networker
- Nurturing
- Obnoxious
- Observant
- Open-Minded
- Optimistic
- Organized
- Patient
- Peaceful
- Persistent
- Picky
- Planner
- Playful
- Poised
- Polite
- Pompous
- Powerful
- Pragmatic
- Precise
- Proactive
- Problem-Solver
- Productive
- Punctual
- Quarrelsome
- Reliable
- Resourceful
- Responsible
- Rude
- Sarcastic
- Self-centered
- Self-confident
- Self-reliant
- Sense of Humor
- Sensual
- Serves Others
- Sincere
- Skillful
- Slovenly
- Sneaky
- Spiritual
- Spontaneous
- Stable
- Stingy
- Strong
- Successful
- Sullen
- Supportive
- Surly
- Tactful
- Thoughtless
- Trusting
- Trusting
- Trustworthy
- Truthful
- Unfriendly
- Unruly
- Versatile
- Vibrant
- Vulgar
- Warm
- Wise
- Zealous

| Name/Nicknames | | Age/Birthday | Race |
|---|---|---|---|
| Height/Weight | Gender/Sexuality | Eyes | Hair color |
| Parents | | Place of Birth | Species |
| Siblings | | Class/Status | Education |
| Where they have lived | | Schools Attended | |
| Clothes/Glasses/Scars | | Spiritual Beliefs | |
| Occupation | | Awards/Accomplishments | |
| Strongest personality characteristics | | Favorite activities/Hobbies | |
| People they love | | People they hate | |
| People they admire | | Pets | Hobbies |
| Problems | | Dreams and Ambitions | |

| Important role in the story | |
|---|---|
| Past experiences that shaped who they are | |
| Character Arc | Notes |

- Accountable
- Adaptable
- Adventurous
- Affable
- Alert
- Ambitious
- Appropriate
- Arrogant
- Assertive
- Astute
- Attentive
- Authentic
- Boorish
- Bossy
- Bravery
- Calm
- Candid
- Capable
- Charismatic
- Charming
- Collaborative
- Committed
- Communicator
- Compassionate
- Conceited
- Confident
- Connected
- Conscientious
- Considerate
- Consistent
- Cooperative
- Courageous
- Cowardly
- Creative
- Cultured
- Curious
- Dedicated
- Dependable
- Determined
- Diplomatic
- Disciplined
- Discreet
- Dishonest
- Dutiful
- Easygoing
- Efficient
- Empathetic
- Encouraging
- Energetic
- Enthusiastic
- Ethical
- Expressive
- Exuberant
- Facilitates
- Fair
- Fairness
- Faithful
- Fearless
- Finicky
- Flexible
- Friendly
- Generative
- Generosity
- Gratitude
- Gregarious
- Happy
- Hard-Working
- Helpful
- Honest
- Honorable
- Humble
- Humorous
- Imaginative
- Immaculate
- Impartial
- Impulsive
- Independent
- Inquiring
- Innovative
- Intelligent
- Intentional
- Interested
- Intimate
- Joyful
- Keen
- Knowledgeable
- Lazy
- Listener
- Lively
- Logical
- Loving
- Loyal
- Malicious
- Meticulous
- Networker
- Nurturing
- Obnoxious
- Observant
- Open-Minded
- Optimistic
- Organized
- Patient
- Peaceful
- Persistent
- Picky
- Planner
- Playful
- Poised
- Polite
- Pompous
- Powerful
- Pragmatic
- Precise
- Proactive
- Problem-Solver
- Productive
- Punctual
- Quarrelsome
- Reliable
- Resourceful
- Responsible
- Rude
- Sarcastic
- Self-centered
- Self-confident
- Self-reliant
- Sense of Humor
- Sensual
- Serves Others
- Sincere
- Skillful
- Slovenly
- Sneaky
- Spiritual
- Spontaneous
- Stable
- Stingy
- Strong
- Successful
- Sullen
- Supportive
- Surly
- Tactful
- Thoughtless
- Trusting
- Trusting
- Trustworthy
- Truthful
- Unfriendly
- Unruly
- Versatile
- Vibrant
- Vulgar
- Warm
- Wise
- Zealous

| Name/Nicknames | | Age/Birthday | Race |
|---|---|---|---|
| Height/Weight | Gender/Sexuality | Eyes | Hair color |
| Parents | | Place of Birth | Species |
| Siblings | | Class/Status | Education |
| Where they have lived | | Schools Attended | |
| Clothes/Glasses/Scars | | Spiritual Beliefs | |
| Occupation | | Awards/Accomplishments | |
| Strongest personality characteristics | | Favorite activities/Hobbies | |
| People they love | | People they hate | |
| People they admire | | Pets | Hobbies |
| Problems | | Dreams and Ambitions | |

| Important role in the story | |
|---|---|
| Past experiences that shaped who they are | |
| Character Arc | Notes |

- ○ Accountable
- ○ Adaptable
- ○ Adventurous
- ○ Affable
- ○ Alert
- ○ Ambitious
- ○ Appropriate
- ○ Arrogant
- ○ Assertive
- ○ Astute
- ○ Attentive
- ○ Authentic
- ○ Boorish
- ○ Bossy
- ○ Bravery
- ○ Calm
- ○ Candid
- ○ Capable
- ○ Charismatic
- ○ Charming
- ○ Collaborative
- ○ Committed
- ○ Communicator
- ○ Compassionate
- ○ Conceited
- ○ Confident
- ○ Connected
- ○ Conscientious
- ○ Considerate
- ○ Consistent
- ○ Cooperative
- ○ Courageous
- ○ Cowardly
- ○ Creative
- ○ Cultured
- ○ Curious
- ○ Dedicated
- ○ Dependable
- ○ Determined
- ○ Diplomatic
- ○ Disciplined
- ○ Discreet
- ○ Dishonest
- ○ Dutiful
- ○ Easygoing
- ○ Efficient
- ○ Empathetic
- ○ Encouraging
- ○ Energetic
- ○ Enthusiastic
- ○ Ethical
- ○ Expressive
- ○ Exuberant
- ○ Facilitates
- ○ Fair
- ○ Fairness
- ○ Faithful
- ○ Fearless
- ○ Finicky
- ○ Flexible
- ○ Friendly
- ○ Generative
- ○ Generosity
- ○ Gratitude
- ○ Gregarious
- ○ Happy
- ○ Hard-Working
- ○ Helpful
- ○ Honest
- ○ Honorable
- ○ Humble
- ○ Humorous
- ○ Imaginative
- ○ Immaculate
- ○ Impartial
- ○ Impulsive
- ○ Independent
- ○ Inquiring
- ○ Innovative
- ○ Intelligent
- ○ Intentional
- ○ Interested
- ○ Intimate
- ○ Joyful
- ○ Keen
- ○ Knowledgeable
- ○ Lazy
- ○ Listener
- ○ Lively
- ○ Logical
- ○ Loving
- ○ Loyal
- ○ Malicious
- ○ Meticulous
- ○ Networker
- ○ Nurturing
- ○ Obnoxious
- ○ Observant
- ○ Open-Minded
- ○ Optimistic
- ○ Organized
- ○ Patient
- ○ Peaceful
- ○ Persistent
- ○ Picky
- ○ Planner
- ○ Playful
- ○ Poised
- ○ Polite
- ○ Pompous
- ○ Powerful
- ○ Pragmatic
- ○ Precise
- ○ Proactive
- ○ Problem-Solver
- ○ Productive
- ○ Punctual
- ○ Quarrelsome
- ○ Reliable
- ○ Resourceful
- ○ Responsible
- ○ Rude
- ○ Sarcastic
- ○ Self-centered
- ○ Self-confident
- ○ Self-reliant
- ○ Sense of Humor
- ○ Sensual
- ○ Serves Others
- ○ Sincere
- ○ Skillful
- ○ Slovenly
- ○ Sneaky
- ○ Spiritual
- ○ Spontaneous
- ○ Stable
- ○ Stingy
- ○ Strong
- ○ Successful
- ○ Sullen
- ○ Supportive
- ○ Surly
- ○ Tactful
- ○ Thoughtless
- ○ Trusting
- ○ Trusting
- ○ Trustworthy
- ○ Truthful
- ○ Unfriendly
- ○ Unruly
- ○ Versatile
- ○ Vibrant
- ○ Vulgar
- ○ Warm
- ○ Wise
- ○ Zealous

| Name/Nicknames | | Age/Birthday | Race |
|---|---|---|---|
| Height/Weight | Gender/Sexuality | Eyes | Hair color |
| Parents | | Place of Birth | Species |
| Siblings | | Class/Status | Education |
| Where they have lived | | Schools Attended | |
| Clothes/Glasses/Scars | | Spiritual Beliefs | |
| Occupation | | Awards/Accomplishments | |
| Strongest personality characteristics | | Favorite activities/Hobbies | |
| People they love | | People they hate | |
| People they admire | | Pets | Hobbies |
| Problems | | Dreams and Ambitions | |

| Important role in the story | |
|---|---|
| Past experiences that shaped who they are | |
| Character Arc | Notes |

- Accountable
- Adaptable
- Adventurous
- Affable
- Alert
- Ambitious
- Appropriate
- Arrogant
- Assertive
- Astute
- Attentive
- Authentic
- Boorish
- Bossy
- Bravery
- Calm
- Candid
- Capable
- Charismatic
- Charming
- Collaborative
- Committed
- Communicator
- Compassionate
- Conceited
- Confident
- Connected
- Conscientious
- Considerate
- Consistent
- Cooperative
- Courageous
- Cowardly
- Creative
- Cultured
- Curious
- Dedicated
- Dependable
- Determined
- Diplomatic
- Disciplined
- Discreet
- Dishonest
- Dutiful
- Easygoing
- Efficient
- Empathetic
- Encouraging
- Energetic
- Enthusiastic
- Ethical
- Expressive
- Exuberant
- Facilitates
- Fair
- Fairness
- Faithful
- Fearless
- Finicky
- Flexible
- Friendly
- Generative
- Generosity
- Gratitude
- Gregarious
- Happy
- Hard-Working
- Helpful
- Honest
- Honorable
- Humble
- Humorous
- Imaginative
- Immaculate
- Impartial
- Impulsive
- Independent
- Inquiring
- Innovative
- Intelligent
- Intentional
- Interested
- Intimate
- Joyful
- Keen
- Knowledgeable
- Lazy
- Listener
- Lively
- Logical
- Loving
- Loyal
- Malicious
- Meticulous
- Networker
- Nurturing
- Obnoxious
- Observant
- Open-Minded
- Optimistic
- Organized
- Patient
- Peaceful
- Persistent
- Picky
- Planner
- Playful
- Poised
- Polite
- Pompous
- Powerful
- Pragmatic
- Precise
- Proactive
- Problem-Solver
- Productive
- Punctual
- Quarrelsome
- Reliable
- Resourceful
- Responsible
- Rude
- Sarcastic
- Self-centered
- Self-confident
- Self-reliant
- Sense of Humor
- Sensual
- Serves Others
- Sincere
- Skillful
- Slovenly
- Sneaky
- Spiritual
- Spontaneous
- Stable
- Stingy
- Strong
- Successful
- Sullen
- Supportive
- Surly
- Tactful
- Thoughtless
- Trusting
- Trusting
- Trustworthy
- Truthful
- Unfriendly
- Unruly
- Versatile
- Vibrant
- Vulgar
- Warm
- Wise
- Zealous

| Name/Nicknames | | Age/Birthday | Race |
|---|---|---|---|
| Height/Weight | Gender/Sexuality | Eyes | Hair color |
| Parents | | Place of Birth | Species |
| Siblings | | Class/Status | Education |
| Where they have lived | | Schools Attended | |
| Clothes/Glasses/Scars | | Spiritual Beliefs | |
| Occupation | | Awards/Accomplishments | |
| Strongest personality characteristics | | Favorite activities/Hobbies | |
| People they love | | People they hate | |
| People they admire | | Pets | Hobbies |
| Problems | | Dreams and Ambitions | |

| | |
|---|---|
| *Important role in the story* | |
| *Past experiences that shaped who they are* | |

| Character Arc | Notes |
|---|---|
| | |

- Accountable
- Adaptable
- Adventurous
- Affable
- Alert
- Ambitious
- Appropriate
- Arrogant
- Assertive
- Astute
- Attentive
- Authentic
- Boorish
- Bossy
- Bravery
- Calm
- Candid
- Capable
- Charismatic
- Charming
- Collaborative
- Committed
- Communicator
- Compassionate
- Conceited
- Confident
- Connected
- Conscientious
- Considerate
- Consistent
- Cooperative
- Courageous
- Cowardly
- Creative
- Cultured
- Curious
- Dedicated
- Dependable
- Determined
- Diplomatic
- Disciplined
- Discreet
- Dishonest
- Dutiful
- Easygoing
- Efficient
- Empathetic
- Encouraging
- Energetic
- Enthusiastic
- Ethical
- Expressive
- Exuberant
- Facilitates
- Fair
- Fairness
- Faithful
- Fearless
- Finicky
- Flexible
- Friendly
- Generative
- Generosity
- Gratitude
- Gregarious
- Happy
- Hard-Working
- Helpful
- Honest
- Honorable
- Humble
- Humorous
- Imaginative
- Immaculate
- Impartial
- Impulsive
- Independent
- Inquiring
- Innovative
- Intelligent
- Intentional
- Interested
- Intimate
- Joyful
- Keen
- Knowledgeable
- Lazy
- Listener
- Lively
- Logical
- Loving
- Loyal
- Malicious
- Meticulous
- Networker
- Nurturing
- Obnoxious
- Observant
- Open-Minded
- Optimistic
- Organized
- Patient
- Peaceful
- Persistent
- Picky
- Planner
- Playful
- Poised
- Polite
- Pompous
- Powerful
- Pragmatic
- Precise
- Proactive
- Problem-Solver
- Productive
- Punctual
- Quarrelsome
- Reliable
- Resourceful
- Responsible
- Rude
- Sarcastic
- Self-centered
- Self-confident
- Self-reliant
- Sense of Humor
- Sensual
- Serves Others
- Sincere
- Skillful
- Slovenly
- Sneaky
- Spiritual
- Spontaneous
- Stable
- Stingy
- Strong
- Successful
- Sullen
- Supportive
- Surly
- Tactful
- Thoughtless
- Trusting
- Trusting
- Trustworthy
- Truthful
- Unfriendly
- Unruly
- Versatile
- Vibrant
- Vulgar
- Warm
- Wise
- Zealous

| Name/Nicknames | | Age/Birthday | Race |
|---|---|---|---|
| Height/Weight | Gender/Sexuality | Eyes | Hair color |
| Parents | | Place of Birth | Species |
| Siblings | | Class/Status | Education |
| Where they have lived | | Schools Attended | |
| Clothes/Glasses/Scars | | Spiritual Beliefs | |
| Occupation | | Awards/Accomplishments | |
| Strongest personality characteristics | | Favorite activities/Hobbies | |
| People they love | | People they hate | |
| People they admire | | Pets | Hobbies |
| Problems | | Dreams and Ambitions | |

| Important role in the story | |
|---|---|
| Past experiences that shaped who they are | |
| Character Arc | Notes |

- Accountable
- Adaptable
- Adventurous
- Affable
- Alert
- Ambitious
- Appropriate
- Arrogant
- Assertive
- Astute
- Attentive
- Authentic
- Boorish
- Bossy
- Bravery
- Calm
- Candid
- Capable
- Charismatic
- Charming
- Collaborative
- Committed
- Communicator
- Compassionate
- Conceited
- Confident
- Connected
- Conscientious
- Considerate
- Consistent
- Cooperative
- Courageous
- Cowardly
- Creative
- Cultured
- Curious
- Dedicated
- Dependable
- Determined
- Diplomatic
- Disciplined
- Discreet
- Dishonest
- Dutiful
- Easygoing
- Efficient
- Empathetic
- Encouraging
- Energetic
- Enthusiastic
- Ethical
- Expressive
- Exuberant
- Facilitates
- Fair
- Fairness
- Faithful
- Fearless
- Finicky
- Flexible
- Friendly
- Generative
- Generosity
- Gratitude
- Gregarious
- Happy
- Hard-Working
- Helpful
- Honest
- Honorable
- Humble
- Humorous
- Imaginative
- Immaculate
- Impartial
- Impulsive
- Independent
- Inquiring
- Innovative
- Intelligent
- Intentional
- Interested
- Intimate
- Joyful
- Keen
- Knowledgeable
- Lazy
- Listener
- Lively
- Logical
- Loving
- Loyal
- Malicious
- Meticulous
- Networker
- Nurturing
- Obnoxious
- Observant
- Open-Minded
- Optimistic
- Organized
- Patient
- Peaceful
- Persistent
- Picky
- Planner
- Playful
- Poised
- Polite
- Pompous
- Powerful
- Pragmatic
- Precise
- Proactive
- Problem-Solver
- Productive
- Punctual
- Quarrelsome
- Reliable
- Resourceful
- Responsible
- Rude
- Sarcastic
- Self-centered
- Self-confident
- Self-reliant
- Sense of Humor
- Sensual
- Serves Others
- Sincere
- Skillful
- Slovenly
- Sneaky
- Spiritual
- Spontaneous
- Stable
- Stingy
- Strong
- Successful
- Sullen
- Supportive
- Surly
- Tactful
- Thoughtless
- Trusting
- Trusting
- Trustworthy
- Truthful
- Unfriendly
- Unruly
- Versatile
- Vibrant
- Vulgar
- Warm
- Wise
- Zealous

| Name/Nicknames | | Age/Birthday | Race |
|---|---|---|---|
| Height/Weight | Gender/Sexuality | Eyes | Hair color |
| Parents | | Place of Birth | Species |
| Siblings | | Class/Status | Education |
| Where they have lived | | Schools Attended | |
| Clothes/Glasses/Scars | | Spiritual Beliefs | |
| Occupation | | Awards/Accomplishments | |
| Strongest personality characteristics | | Favorite activities/Hobbies | |
| People they love | | People they hate | |
| People they admire | | Pets | Hobbies |
| Problems | | Dreams and Ambitions | |

| Important role in the story | |
|---|---|
| Past experiences that shaped who they are | |

| Character Arc | Notes |
|---|---|
| | |

- Accountable
- Adaptable
- Adventurous
- Affable
- Alert
- Ambitious
- Appropriate
- Arrogant
- Assertive
- Astute
- Attentive
- Authentic
- Boorish
- Bossy
- Bravery
- Calm
- Candid
- Capable
- Charismatic
- Charming
- Collaborative
- Committed
- Communicator
- Compassionate
- Conceited
- Confident
- Connected
- Conscientious
- Considerate
- Consistent
- Cooperative
- Courageous
- Cowardly
- Creative
- Cultured
- Curious
- Dedicated
- Dependable
- Determined
- Diplomatic
- Disciplined
- Discreet
- Dishonest
- Dutiful
- Easygoing
- Efficient
- Empathetic
- Encouraging
- Energetic
- Enthusiastic
- Ethical
- Expressive
- Exuberant
- Facilitates
- Fair
- Fairness
- Faithful
- Fearless
- Finicky
- Flexible
- Friendly
- Generative
- Generosity
- Gratitude
- Gregarious
- Happy
- Hard-Working
- Helpful
- Honest
- Honorable
- Humble
- Humorous
- Imaginative
- Immaculate
- Impartial
- Impulsive
- Independent
- Inquiring
- Innovative
- Intelligent
- Intentional
- Interested
- Intimate
- Joyful
- Keen
- Knowledgeable
- Lazy
- Listener
- Lively
- Logical
- Loving
- Loyal
- Malicious
- Meticulous
- Networker
- Nurturing
- Obnoxious
- Observant
- Open-Minded
- Optimistic
- Organized
- Patient
- Peaceful
- Persistent
- Picky
- Planner
- Playful
- Poised
- Polite
- Pompous
- Powerful
- Pragmatic
- Precise
- Proactive
- Problem-Solver
- Productive
- Punctual
- Quarrelsome
- Reliable
- Resourceful
- Responsible
- Rude
- Sarcastic
- Self-centered
- Self-confident
- Self-reliant
- Sense of Humor
- Sensual
- Serves Others
- Sincere
- Skillful
- Slovenly
- Sneaky
- Spiritual
- Spontaneous
- Stable
- Stingy
- Strong
- Successful
- Sullen
- Supportive
- Surly
- Tactful
- Thoughtless
- Trusting
- Trusting
- Trustworthy
- Truthful
- Unfriendly
- Unruly
- Versatile
- Vibrant
- Vulgar
- Warm
- Wise
- Zealous

| Name/Nicknames | | Age/Birthday | Race |
| --- | --- | --- | --- |
| Height/Weight | Gender/Sexuality | Eyes | Hair color |
| Parents | | Place of Birth | Species |
| Siblings | | Class/Status | Education |
| Where they have lived | | Schools Attended | |
| Clothes/Glasses/Scars | | Spiritual Beliefs | |
| Occupation | | Awards/Accomplishments | |
| Strongest personality characteristics | | Favorite activities/Hobbies | |
| People they love | | People they hate | |
| People they admire | | Pets | Hobbies |
| Problems | | Dreams and Ambitions | |

| Important role in the story | |
|---|---|
| Past experiences that shaped who they are | |

| Character Arc | Notes |
|---|---|

- ○ Accountable
- ○ Adaptable
- ○ Adventurous
- ○ Affable
- ○ Alert
- ○ Ambitious
- ○ Appropriate
- ○ Arrogant
- ○ Assertive
- ○ Astute
- ○ Attentive
- ○ Authentic
- ○ Boorish
- ○ Bossy
- ○ Bravery
- ○ Calm
- ○ Candid
- ○ Capable
- ○ Charismatic
- ○ Charming
- ○ Collaborative
- ○ Committed
- ○ Communicator
- ○ Compassionate
- ○ Conceited
- ○ Confident
- ○ Connected
- ○ Conscientious
- ○ Considerate
- ○ Consistent
- ○ Cooperative
- ○ Courageous
- ○ Cowardly
- ○ Creative
- ○ Cultured
- ○ Curious
- ○ Dedicated
- ○ Dependable
- ○ Determined

- ○ Diplomatic
- ○ Disciplined
- ○ Discreet
- ○ Dishonest
- ○ Dutiful
- ○ Easygoing
- ○ Efficient
- ○ Empathetic
- ○ Encouraging
- ○ Energetic
- ○ Enthusiastic
- ○ Ethical
- ○ Expressive
- ○ Exuberant
- ○ Facilitates
- ○ Fair
- ○ Fairness
- ○ Faithful
- ○ Fearless
- ○ Finicky
- ○ Flexible
- ○ Friendly
- ○ Generative
- ○ Generosity
- ○ Gratitude
- ○ Gregarious
- ○ Happy
- ○ Hard-Working
- ○ Helpful
- ○ Honest
- ○ Honorable
- ○ Humble
- ○ Humorous
- ○ Imaginative
- ○ Immaculate
- ○ Impartial
- ○ Impulsive
- ○ Independent
- ○ Inquiring

- ○ Innovative
- ○ Intelligent
- ○ Intentional
- ○ Interested
- ○ Intimate
- ○ Joyful
- ○ Keen
- ○ Knowledgeable
- ○ Lazy
- ○ Listener
- ○ Lively
- ○ Logical
- ○ Loving
- ○ Loyal
- ○ Malicious
- ○ Meticulous
- ○ Networker
- ○ Nurturing
- ○ Obnoxious
- ○ Observant
- ○ Open-Minded
- ○ Optimistic
- ○ Organized
- ○ Patient
- ○ Peaceful
- ○ Persistent
- ○ Picky
- ○ Planner
- ○ Playful
- ○ Poised
- ○ Polite
- ○ Pompous
- ○ Powerful
- ○ Pragmatic
- ○ Precise
- ○ Proactive
- ○ Problem-Solver
- ○ Productive
- ○ Punctual

- ○ Quarrelsome
- ○ Reliable
- ○ Resourceful
- ○ Responsible
- ○ Rude
- ○ Sarcastic
- ○ Self-centered
- ○ Self-confident
- ○ Self-reliant
- ○ Sense of Humor
- ○ Sensual
- ○ Serves Others
- ○ Sincere
- ○ Skillful
- ○ Slovenly
- ○ Sneaky
- ○ Spiritual
- ○ Spontaneous
- ○ Stable
- ○ Stingy
- ○ Strong
- ○ Successful
- ○ Sullen
- ○ Supportive
- ○ Surly
- ○ Tactful
- ○ Thoughtless
- ○ Trusting
- ○ Trusting
- ○ Trustworthy
- ○ Truthful
- ○ Unfriendly
- ○ Unruly
- ○ Versatile
- ○ Vibrant
- ○ Vulgar
- ○ Warm
- ○ Wise
- ○ Zealous

| Name/Nicknames | | Age/Birthday | Race |
|---|---|---|---|
| Height/Weight | Gender/Sexuality | Eyes | Hair color |
| Parents | | Place of Birth | Species |
| Siblings | | Class/Status | Education |
| Where they have lived | | Schools Attended | |
| Clothes/Glasses/Scars | | Spiritual Beliefs | |
| Occupation | | Awards/Accomplishments | |
| Strongest personality characteristics | | Favorite activities/Hobbies | |
| People they love | | People they hate | |
| People they admire | | Pets | Hobbies |
| Problems | | Dreams and Ambitions | |

| Important role in the story | |
|---|---|
| Past experiences that shaped who they are | |

| Character Arc | Notes |
|---|---|
| | |

| | | | |
|---|---|---|---|
| o Accountable | o Diplomatic | o Innovative | o Quarrelsome |
| o Adaptable | o Disciplined | o Intelligent | o Reliable |
| o Adventurous | o Discreet | o Intentional | o Resourceful |
| o Affable | o Dishonest | o Interested | o Responsible |
| o Alert | o Dutiful | o Intimate | o Rude |
| o Ambitious | o Easygoing | o Joyful | o Sarcastic |
| o Appropriate | o Efficient | o Keen | o Self-centered |
| o Arrogant | o Empathetic | o Knowledgeable | o Self-confident |
| o Assertive | o Encouraging | o Lazy | o Self-reliant |
| o Astute | o Energetic | o Listener | o Sense of Humor |
| o Attentive | o Enthusiastic | o Lively | o Sensual |
| o Authentic | o Ethical | o Logical | o Serves Others |
| o Boorish | o Expressive | o Loving | o Sincere |
| o Bossy | o Exuberant | o Loyal | o Skillful |
| o Bravery | o Facilitates | o Malicious | o Slovenly |
| o Calm | o Fair | o Meticulous | o Sneaky |
| o Candid | o Fairness | o Networker | o Spiritual |
| o Capable | o Faithful | o Nurturing | o Spontaneous |
| o Charismatic | o Fearless | o Obnoxious | o Stable |
| o Charming | o Finicky | o Observant | o Stingy |
| o Collaborative | o Flexible | o Open-Minded | o Strong |
| o Committed | o Friendly | o Optimistic | o Successful |
| o Communicator | o Generative | o Organized | o Sullen |
| o Compassionate | o Generosity | o Patient | o Supportive |
| o Conceited | o Gratitude | o Peaceful | o Surly |
| o Confident | o Gregarious | o Persistent | o Tactful |
| o Connected | o Happy | o Picky | o Thoughtless |
| o Conscientious | o Hard-Working | o Planner | o Trusting |
| o Considerate | o Helpful | o Playful | o Trusting |
| o Consistent | o Honest | o Poised | o Trustworthy |
| o Cooperative | o Honorable | o Polite | o Truthful |
| o Courageous | o Humble | o Pompous | o Unfriendly |
| o Cowardly | o Humorous | o Powerful | o Unruly |
| o Creative | o Imaginative | o Pragmatic | o Versatile |
| o Cultured | o Immaculate | o Precise | o Vibrant |
| o Curious | o Impartial | o Proactive | o Vulgar |
| o Dedicated | o Impulsive | o Problem-Solver | o Warm |
| o Dependable | o Independent | o Productive | o Wise |
| o Determined | o Inquiring | o Punctual | o Zealous |

www.ingramcontent.com/pod-product-compliance
Lightning Source LLC
Chambersburg PA
CBHW051807100526
44592CB00016B/2601